Agents
of Change

Agents
of Change
Managing the Introduction
of Automated Tools

BARBARA M. BOULDIN

YOURDON PRESS
Prentice Hall Building
Englewood Cliffs, NJ 07632

Library of Congress Cataloging-in-Publication Data

BOULDIN, BARBARA M.
 Agents of change.

 Bibliography: p. 188
 Includes index.
 1. Management—Data processing. 2. Technological
innovations—Management. 3. Organizational change.
I. Title.
HD30.2.B68 1989   658'.05   88-31635
ISBN 0-13-018508-6

Editorial/production supervision
  and interior design: Rob DeGeorge
Cover design: Ben Santora
Manufacturing buyer: Mary Ann Gloriande

 ©1989 by Prentice-Hall, Inc.
A Division of Simon & Schuster
Englewood Cliffs, New Jersey 07632

The publisher offers discounts on this book when ordered
in bulk quantities. For more information, write:

> Special Sales/College Marketing
> Prentice-Hall, Inc.
> College Technical and Reference Division
> Englewood Cliffs, NJ 07632

Printed in the United States of America

10 9 8 7 6 5 4 3 2 1

ISBN 0-13-018508-6

PRENTICE-HALL INTERNATIONAL (UK) LIMITED, *London*
PRENTICE-HALL OF AUSTRALIA PTY. LIMITED, *Sydney*
PRENTICE-HALL CANADA INC., *Toronto*
PRENTICE-HALL HISPANOAMERICANA, S.A., *Mexico*
PRENTICE-HALL OF INDIA PRIVATE LIMITED, *New Delhi*
PRENTICE-HALL OF JAPAN, INC., *Tokyo*
SIMON & SCHUSTER ASIA PTE. LTD., *Singapore*
EDITORA PRENTICE-HALL DO BRASIL, LTDA., *Rio de Janeiro*

This book is dedicated
to Dorr, Adam,
and Karen.

The following are registered trademarks:

Excelerator
UNIX
Lightyear
PW
GWBASIC
MS-DOS
VI
NORTON UTILITIES (ADVANCED)

Contents

Foreword

For the past ten years, the data processing profession has been slowly learning that *technology transfer* is one its biggest problems—if not *the* biggest problem. We have lived through a bewildering array of new hardware and software technologies, most of which are supposed to increase the productivity of the average programmer and systems analyst by a factor of ten or more; yet these technologies are not even being used in many DP organizations and have achieved only modest results in many others.

Does this mean that fourth generation languages, Computer-Aided Software Engineering, structured analysis, and dozens of other technologies don't work. No, it just means that it's difficult to get people—even programmers and analysts, who work with leading-edge hardware technology every day—to make major changes in the way they do their work. We should not be surprised by this; the same technology transfer problem has occurred in other fields, too. It took the military 75 years to go from the technology of muskets to the technology of rifles, so we should not be too discouraged to learn that it takes 14–15 years (according to a report presented in a recent software engineering conference) for new software technologies to be accepted.

Why does it take so long? Because 80% of the staff is working on maintenance projects and has no opportunity to use new technologies of any kind. Because the rest of the staff is working on a "crunch mode" project and they're too far behind schedule to take the time to learn a new method of developing systems. Because the person who introduced the new technology has little or no political clout and even less communication skills. Because nobody has presented senior management with any convincing evidence about the economics of the new technology.

Now that everyone is beginning to appreciate the magnitude of the technology transfer problem, an obvious question is being raised: "How do we solve the technology transfer problem? How can we actually implement a new technology in our organization?" For a consultant in the DP field, such a question is an open invitation for an extended consulting assignment; but for a long time, there was little or nothing written about the subject of technology transfer.

And that's where Barbara Bouldin's book, *Agents of Change*, comes in. Ms. Bouldin has not only talked about successfully implementing technology transfer, she's done it. And she's done it not just for a trivial piece of technology in a small company where all of the programmers could fit in one conference room. She has done it with CASE tools and data modeling methodologies in the largest company in the country, AT&T. This is a woman who knows what she is talking about; if you're trying to implement structured analysis, or JAD, or some new prototyping approach in *your* company, you had better read what she has to say.

You'll find, as you read through this book, that Ms. Bouldin deals almost exclusively with "people issues." She explains how to deal with personalities: the personalities of your bosses, and *their* bosses; the personalities of your peers; the personalities of the "users" to whom you are introducing this new technology; and the personalities of the other members of your team. (There is an implicit assumption that it takes more than one person to implement a new technology in a large organization and the author assumes that you, the reader, are the manager of a team of people charged with the responsibility of implementing a new technology.)

Much of what Ms. Bouldin has to say in *Agents of Change* may seem like common sense; but it isn't really common sense until after you have read it. If you are at all honest, you will have to admit to yourself as you read through each chapter, "Well, that's obvious ... but I wonder if I would have thought of it on my own in time to deal with the situation?" Here's an example: Ms. Bouldin points out that you should be prepared, in the midst of installing your new technology, for a major management reorganization. The reorganization will probably not have anything to do with the work you are doing (indeed, it probably won't be attributable to anything; reorganizations are just a random but necessary occurrence in large organizations). However, it means that you will have a new boss to deal with, as well as the possibility of several new faces at your level and at your boss's level. All of those people whom you had carefully "sold" on the benefits of your new technology and your plan for implementing it, may need to be sold again.

Perhaps the best evidence of the author's practical experience in this field is her emphasis—four chapters of material—on "finishing up" the implementation of a new technology. These chapters not only deal with the possibilities of disasters but also advise the reader on how to handle success. What do you do *after* you have successfully implemented a new technology in your DP organization? It's a question that most technical people haven't even considered. Ms. Bouldin has not only thought about it but has lived through it.

People resist change. Even data processing people resist change. Ironically, sometimes they resist change even more than the end-users to whom they constantly introduce new systems. If you are going to introduce major changes in your DP organization, you're going to need a lot of help and advice. I can't think of a better way to begin than by reading Barbara Bouldin's *Agents of Change*.

Ed Yourdon

Preface

The data processing industry is about to undergo a significant transformation. Consider the fact that a steadily increasing share of the corporate budget is dedicated to data processing and the major portion of that money is directed to production and maintenance. Many top executives, in small as well as large corporations, have begun clamoring for their DP managers to improve productivity. For survival in a field that will soon be unrecognizable, it is essential for professionals to be able to introduce new technologies to their organizations.

This is not a book about heroics or superstars with advanced degrees in computer science who are on a glamorous development project; it is about large IS organizations enhancing and maintaining systems that have been in production for many years. It is about real people who are trying to survive the pressures that accompany such an environment. They are managers, project leaders, systems analysts, and programmers who are no longer willing to suffer through the cost of the successes, not to mention the horrors of the failures. As the industry comes to maturity, so do the professionals that comprise it, and they have begun to search for solutions.

During previous decades, leaders in the industry developed techniques (such as structured systems analysis) that would enable us to produce quality software. It was, however, very difficult to apply these techniques successfully under the time constraints of typical systems development. But during the last several years we have witnessed the development of tools like CASE that mechanize these techniques. What has occurred with the advent of these tools is that it is now possible for us to utilize the techniques that produce quality software.

However, although techniques and technology are now available, the limiting factor is people themselves; there is a natural tendency on the part of all humans to resist change. This book describes a multitude of forms this resistance can assume and offers practical advice on overcoming the resistance painlessly. Moreover, there is a notable lack of practical and immediately applicable information available on the subject of introducing new technology. Theories abound in copious volumes which no person currently active in the field of data processing has the time or energy to read.

This book offers one-stop-shopping for managing the entire process of implementing automated tools. A wide variety of topics is covered in a manner that is conversational and fun! The intent is that *Agents of Change* will supply the required information in an enjoyable manner. Then overworked people may actually find time and energy to read and learn about techniques they can apply the next day on the job.

Barbara Bouldin

Acknowledgments

To my husband, Dorr Bouldin, who believed in me always. He freely gave his support during the writing of *Agents of Change* as well as unstinting assistance during its production.

To my children, Karen and Adam Butler, and my stepson, Matthew Bouldin, for gracefully surviving my distraction while I wrote this book.

To my parents, Alma and Herbert Kaufman, who indisputably had the greatest influence on my development into an agent of change.

To my beloved grandmother, Till Kaufman, a self-made business woman, who inspired me with her spirit and courage to set seemingly impossible goals.

To Ed Yourdon, who not only provided considerable advice but also faith that I could undertake the writing of a book.

To Tom Cooper, who was not only my boss and mentor but will undoubtedly recognize many of the ideas and insights.

To Dale Smith, who when he was my boss transformed me from an analyst to a manager.

To Malcolm Marks, who showed me the true way that people learn and change.

To Peter Brennan, who provided opportunities and the confidence to take them.

To all the people who offered support in a variety of ways—from providing software to encouragement; but especially to: Gertrude Scott, Brenda Rogers, Tom Finneran, Loraine and Warner Bouldin, Berniece Alexander, Carol and Tom Mussel, Chris Murray, Carol Czuko, Chris Grejtak, and Jesse Solodar.

To all the people who provided input and commentary as this book evolved; but especially to Mary Craven, Karen Way, Jack Kearns, Jerry Grochow, Bill Bruyn, Sylvia Kirkland, Fran Collier, and George Dorer.

To all the people at Prentice-Hall who helped me take a series of word processor files and produce a book; but especially to Ed Moura, Rob DeGeorge, Jeannine Ciliotta, and Charles Decker.

To all my friends at AT&T and Bell Laboratories, with whom I have worked through the years; but especially to Mary Silver, who supported me throughout the writing of this book and was also my first fellow change agent.

Agents
of Change

Assessing the Need

In a world that is becoming increasingly mechanized, we as data processing professionals have not placed significant emphasis on improving how we perform our own jobs. Although we have spent decades automating the manual processes of virtually every other profession, we have only recently turned our attention to what I term "mechanization of the mechanizers."

MECHANIZATION OF THE MECHANIZERS

Recently considerable attention has been given to productivity in our profession. There are several compelling reasons for this belated attention. The most significant reason is directly related to the maturity of data processing as an industry, as well as the increasing maturity of the individuals who comprise it. We are no longer bright-eyed young kids right out of college, brimming with energy and enthusiasm. On the contrary, we have all been through development of countless systems and if we don't know the perfect way to engineer software, we surely know what we would like to avoid. We have had a lifetime quota of bringing up systems both behind schedule and over budget that do not begin to satisfy their users.

In fact, we are beginning to question the cost of our successes. Remember the last "successful" system you developed; the one that was on time, within budget, and appreciated by the users. You will probably also recall that this was the time when you did not see your family or friends for days on end, your project leader developed an ulcer, and your technical guru resigned! We are beginning to ask ourselves not only "How many times can we go through this?" but also "Is it worth any reward?" Therefore, it is not particularly astonishing that many of us are now actively seeking relief by searching for better ways to develop systems.

Considering the increasing share of the corporate budget that is dedicated to data processing, it is also not surprising that there is increasing pressure to rectify any inefficiencies in system development and maintenance. In many companies, small as well as large, top executives have begun to take an active interest in the problem. The result of all this heightened awareness is an ever-growing industry that is comprised of a wide variety and assortment of tools and techniques that purport to improve productivity.

DIFFICULTY OF A TECHNOLOGY TRANSFER

However, even though it would seem that the time is right to mechanize the jobs associated with developing software, this "mechanization of the mechanizers" does not appear to be a totally smooth evolution. The average person in any area of data processing is not only usually overworked and behind schedule, but now also faces a steady barrage of new technology, theories, methodologies, and tools. Moreover, due to economic considerations, it is not uncommon for top management to adopt one of the increasingly popular computer-aided software engineering (CASE) tools as a solution to everyone's collective problems.

Some of these innovations are helpful and some are not but usually no one has given any thought to whether or not the products are appropriate for a particular organization or company. The difficulties of implementing a new technology have very little to do with the quality of the product itself; rather, they are related to the intangible but real obstacles associated with overcoming resistance. This resistance implies that the rate of technology transfer is directly related to the ability of the agents of change to gain acceptance from their users. Thus data processing managers and their employees are quickly discovering that in order to improve productivity, they must invest in more than a tool or technique. In those groups that manage to achieve substantial improvement, a fundamental change in attitude occurs that borders on a cultural revolution.

THE MISSION

Several years ago, I set out on a crusade. Management declared me a missionary and commanded me to go forth and convert everyone in our organization. The religion I was preaching involved embracing the concept of productivity in the form of an automated software tool called Excelerator. As far as I can decipher their motives, my management selected me because I was a true believer; in other words, I was the first convert.

Given the hype associated with CASE at the time, I was positive that everyone in the data processing industry had productivity as a high priority. I believed that the beleaguered managers as well as their staffs would welcome major changes in their daily work life. Needless to say, I was in for a real surprise. Although most managers and their employees consider productivity an objective, it is almost never a priority. A priority is putting in a production fix by 6:00 A.M. the following day or meeting a deadline for the next release. Changing how you perform the activities that comprise your job so that the quality of your systems and your daily life is improved was viewed as a luxury or even a nuisance.

At that stage of my data processing career, I already had considerable savvy, having progressed through the years from a development staff member to the management ranks. I quickly assimilated the message that was being communicated and retreated to rethink my position. Many thoughts came to mind, not the least of which was that I still believed (with all the fervor of a convert) in achieving our original objective: implementing a CASE tool to improve productivity. The year that followed made an indelible impression on me and on my management. We succeeded in our implementation—not as rapidly and dramatically as we had envisioned, but perhaps with more thoroughness and acceptance than anyone had anticipated.

THE LIFE CYCLE OF IMPLEMENTING CHANGE

Afterward as I reflected upon the approach we took and the techniques we employed, it occurred to me that this was far from the first time I had traveled this particular road. Moreover, the more I analyzed and compared previous change efforts to the current one, I realized not only that we had become increasingly adept at implementing change, but also that we tended to follow the same steps and techniques for every effort. Given the sequence of events and my analysis of them, I arrived at the only possible conclusion: Just as there is a life cycle for developing software, so too there is a life cycle for implementing change (see Figure 1–1).

Moreover, it is my firm conviction that the basic structure, activities, and approach will be the same for implementing any change. Although there may be differences at the detail level, no matter what product you have chosen as your vehicle for improvement, the phases of effecting change will be as follows:

Assessing the need
Selecting the candidate products
Evaluating the products
Presenting the product
Gathering information
Planning the implementation
Implementing change
Finishing the implementation

It is the objective of *Agents of Change* to describe each phase in great detail and to provide examples (failures as well as successes) based on the experiences

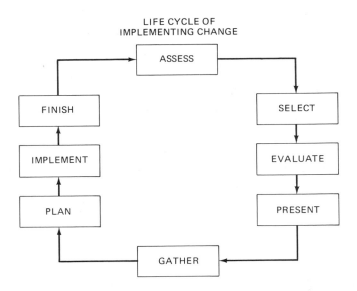

Figure 1-1 The phases of implementing change are always exactly the same and therefore are independent of a particular technology that is being introduced.

(real, composite, and apocryphal) of myself and my fellow change agents. Since the process was not revolutionary or dramatic, it can provide assistance to any manager (at any level in the organizational hierarchy), project leader, or systems analyst. Thus, it is now possible for many data processing professionals to become change agents and to successfully implement new techniques and tools in their own environments.

IS THE TIME RIGHT?

The very first step, before you even begin to search for productivity tools or techniques, is to determine whether or not the time is right for your environment. This seems like a vague and insurmountable task; however, there are signs for which you can search. Here is a test that you can take on behalf of your department that will help you make the determination. Answer the questions with your initial reaction; this will reveal the propensity to accept change at this particular time.

1. Is your organization newly formed?
2. Are the functions your organization performs new to your corporation?
3. Is your organization growing at a reasonably rapid rate?
4. Is your organization responsible for the development of new systems?
5. Is there a general attitude of optimism, and is morale high?

6. Are your analysts and programmers utilizing tools or methods that improve productivity?
7. Does your management support the concept of productivity in any way?
8. Is the staff experiencing motivation problems?
9. Is your organization responsible for mature systems that are primarily in a maintenance mode?
10. Does your organization have a backlog of user requests without enough resources to implement most of them?

Your answers and what they indicate may surprise you and you may even seriously question whether you can adequately represent your organization. However, the intent of this self-test is to assess attitudes, and your responses should accurately reflect the attitude of any organization of which you are a longstanding member. For example, you may have wondered whether productivity in this context could include an on-line debug facility or whether it must be something as complex as the newest system test tool on the market. That train of thought is not even relevant, because having a precise definition firmly in mind is unimportant. What is essential is that as a whole your organization believes it is already implementing productivity improvement measures.

Now let's turn to the actual items of the self-test. If you answered most of the first five questions "yes," then you probably should delay introducing productivity improvement measures. This suggestion may not be what you anticipated. In fact, many people do attempt to interject productivity improvements at the outset of a new project or when a new organization is forming. Our experience indicates that this may be far from the optimal time. Remember the first few development projects on which you were a team member? It is unlikely that you were interested in the myriad of planning meetings that took place between the project manager and the users. Nor was it probable that you had much patience with the time and resource negotiations that slowly evolved into Gantt and Pert charts. You wanted to design, to code, and to build a system! In fact, during the last project for which you were responsible that involved leading edge technology, you may have experienced some similar (and almost forgotten) stirrings of impatience. You found yourself silently questioning the slowness with which your management, users, vendors, etc. were moving; you (jaded as you were) wanted to have an opportunity to play with the new toy.

A new organization is imbued with vitality; a team embarking on the development of a new system is usually bristling with enthusiasm. Therefore, in these types of environments, it is unlikely that you will be able to get anyone to stop what they are doing long enough to even spell the word productivity. Your suggestions will probably be received better if you approach people after they have missed a few critical deadlines and are beginning to feel discouraged. At that point most people are actively searching for relief, which you can supply.

On the other hand, if you answered "yes" to most of the last five questions on the self-test, the time is indeed right! Your group has been through the wars and are most definitely battle weary. The members are past the first flush of optimism and all-consuming interest in what they are doing from a technological perspective. They are unbearably familiar with their systems' shortcomings and are definitely fed up with resolving production problems by phone at 3:00 A.M. In some cases, they may be searching for ways to improve how they implement new releases; these are the groups that are already utilizing productivity tools or techniques. These are the people who will be in an excellent position to appreciate the benefits of the productivity improvement you will recommend.

LOOK WITHIN YOURSELF

Obviously, arriving at this determination is not an exact science and even the act of utilizing the ten questions may be somewhat less than straightforward. Therefore, a diagram (Figure 1–2) has been provided to help you summarize your answers as well as analyze their significance. You may also notice that there is a third possibility; namely, the case where you answered "yes" to most questions or "no" to most questions.

   If this is your situation, then it will be somewhat more difficult to assess the prevailing climate of your organization. In this case you must look deep within yourself and trust your instincts. We can, however, offer some additional questions that might assist you with this self-assessment. Ask yourself: If your recommendations are accepted and the results are unfavorable, would this dramatically

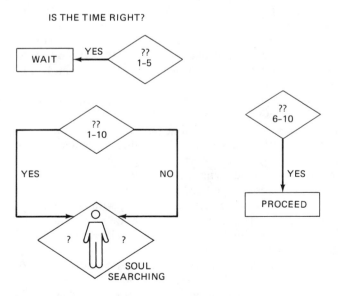

Figure 1–2 A schematic for analyzing the ten questions.

and adversely affect your position in the organization? Then you must also evaluate not only how much you really believe in the cause you have selected, but also exactly what you are willing to risk.

The key things to consider are the possible adverse effects on your career, your own level of commitment, and the extent of the potential improvement. You are the only one who can assess these factors. Do bear in mind, however, the seriousness of what you are about to undertake. It is not at all in the same category as typical advice to the boss, such as sending the new programmer to a course halfway across the country. You will be recommending something that if it is approved, will result in a considerable expenditure of funds; and more important, if it is successful, will have far-reaching effects on many people. You must fully understand and appreciate the tremendous implications of the fact that you are about to change irrevocably how people perform their jobs.

In order to succeed, you must begin with firm convictions, based on a realistic appraisal of the situation. Specifically, you must also assess yourself as part of the whole process, because as an agent of change, you will definitely be a critical success factor. How comfortable do you really feel with the new tool, technique, etc.? Do you truly believe it is really going to make a dramatic difference (in terms of quality and time) in how systems are developed in your organization? Is this a good time (in terms of career) for you to be taking such a risk? If you have the impression that your prospects of promotion in the near future are bleak, advocating this type of change may be perfect. Although your efforts may not result in any specific reward, at least you will not forfeit something positive that is imminent. However, you should never be unduly influenced by political considerations. If the tool or technique is fundamentally a good product that will substantially improve development and you fervently believe those two facts, then by all means you should recommend it. But never forget that you are a missionary on a crusade, and that one prerequisite for successful implementation of change is a zealot.

SELECT A TARGET AREA FOR IMPROVEMENT

You surely do not want to proceed with a major change effort if you can foresee only minimal improvement. There is absolutely no advantage to implementing change for its own sake. Therefore, before you proceed, you must be confident that the tools or techniques will substantially improve the situation at this time. The first step to determining this fact is to size up the entire development process in which your organization is involved. Select an area or phase (e.g., system definition) in which you can clearly see problems. The following list offers some common problems, and you should use it as a checklist. However, do not limit yourself to these items; add your own to the list so it will be more applicable to your organization.

1. Repeated inability to meet target dates for this phase
2. Low morale among group members during this phase

3. Redundant activities and/or documents produced
4. Constant false starts—the let's go back to the drawing board syndrome (once is not an indication)
5. Inability to get started at all
6. Specific sets of activities or tasks repeatedly performed
7. Tasks performed inadvertently by more than one group member
8. Critical tasks not performed
9. In general, a lack of communication and control

Utilizing the problems you have identified, you will then select the phase or area targeted for improvement. Following that activity, spend a modest amount of time in reflection. Try to imagine the ideal situation—activities being performed in an atmosphere of cooperation, energetically but without hysteria, by competent team members who meet all deadlines with all deliverables. Now that you have the two pictures (current and ideal) firmly in mind, compare them as honestly as possible. It should be clear to you that the current and ideal scenarios are qualitatively and thus substantially different. If not, then it is not clear that the gain will be worth the effort.

QUANTIFY THE PROJECTED BENEFITS

This "imaging" is a bit like a trip to the ether zone, so we will offer a more concrete method that we have used in determining whether to proceed or delay. This approach involves quantifying the projected benefits as a step in the assessment process. This does not have to be a formal business case, but just a simple analysis of the situation that you will be improving in terms of dollars and cents. Bear in mind that there are many ways to perform cost/benefit analysis, some of which are quite complicated; and the method we will describe is an unsophisticated one.

Utilizing the two scenarios you have just mentally developed, apply the following technique. Take the target phase as it exists in both the current and idealized versions, and attach dollar figures to both scenarios. This is accomplished by compiling a list of necessary activities and determining the number of people and average amount of time required to complete these activities. Then you can calculate the cost by multiplying these figures by loaded salaries (usually you can obtain these figures from personnel). For example:

For a system test, your project usually takes two months and assigns six people.

Three of these people are senior members of your programming staff (MPS) with a loaded salary of $60,000 per year; the other three are junior members of your programming staff with a loaded salary of $40,000 per year.

Therefore, if your system test lasted for a year, you would spend:

Senior MPS		Junior MPS		Total
$3 \times \$60,000$	$+$	$3 \times \$40,000$	$=$	$\$300,000$

Since your system test period usually takes two months, you usually spend:

$$1/6 \text{ of } \$300,000 = \$50,000 \text{ per release}$$

If you have two releases per year on the average

$$2 \times \$50,000 = \$100,000 \text{ per year on system test.}$$

In the ideal situation, you predict that the three junior MPS, armed with a productivity measure, could do the job in the same amount of time. Therefore, if your system test lasted for a year, it would cost:

$$3 \times \$40,000 = \$120,000 \text{ per year}$$

or

$$1/6 \text{ of } \$120,000 = \$20,0000 \text{ per release}$$

Again, if you usually have two releases per year:

$$2 \times \$20,000 = \$40,000 \text{ per year on system test}$$

Thus, your projected savings would be:

$$\$100,000 - \$40,000 = \$60,000 \text{ per year}$$

You should also consider other expenses such as the computer costs (purchase, lease, or timeshare) for the duration of the system test. If this is a substantial expense for your group, this calculation will improve your projected savings. Moreover, if you already have a particular tool or methodology in mind, you must include the cost of the tool itself. If it is very expensive (some tools may cost $500,000 or more), and your projections indicate approximate savings of $25,000 per year, it would take years to recoup the initial expenditure. In this case you would probably not want to proceed with your recommendation. However, although you need to be careful, you should not be too cautious. If the tool would be used many times a year by several groups, then a very large initial expenditure may still be worthwhile.

After you have followed the steps outlined in the preceding paragraphs, you must analyze the results very carefully (Figure 1–3 offers a pictorial summary). Even though these estimates are usually never seen by anyone other than you, it is important to be very conservative. In general, you will be pleasantly surprised; there is no advantage in setting yourself up for a disappointment. Keep in mind that the main reason you are projecting these figures is to enable you to address whether or not the improvement would be substantial. All this quantification will bring some objectivity to an otherwise extremely subjective issue. Your management will feel much more comfortable if you feel confident in your advocacy of the new tool or technique.

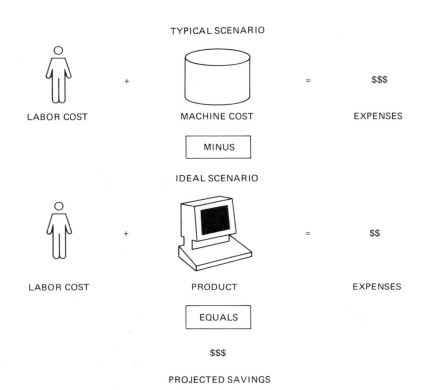

Figure 1–3   A pictorial summary of the quantification process.

However, if your analysis leads to the conclusion that you should stop based on the economics, so be it. But don't despair—situations change, people change, and the time will be right eventually, probably after a few more releases of the system or after the new organization matures. In any case, you should save your figures, because you may want to recalculate the quantifications as the environment evolves. At any time (now or in the future), if your estimates indicate a promising area for productivity improvement, you will proceed and you can use these figures as a basis for your business case.

WHEN TO SHOW YOUR HAND

By now you have assessed your organization as well as yourself, and you have determined that the time is right. You are also confident that the benefits will be substantial, and you are indeed committed. But there is still one question to ask yourself before this phase is complete: You must consider not only the advisability of sharing your plans at this time, but also the extent to which they should be shared and with whom. It may not be obvious, but you actually will have quite a bit of latitude in terms of when your crusade becomes public knowledge. Although this may seem trivial, there are a number of reasons that this flexibility cannot be disregarded.

Once, in the early days of distributed processing, we conceived of an application that would support all our system documentation from definition to user guides. We envisioned that our "paperless environment" would operate on a two-tier architecture and developed a comprehensive prototype. The need existed, the time was right, and we were crusaders; however, we made the fatal error of communicating our mission to the free world. Our technical support group claimed ownership, since the technology was leading edge; the project group across the hall unequivocally stated that the functionality was redundant due to the scope of their effort; the corporate groups informed us that what we produced was not SOE (standard operating environment). In fact, our own management questioned our priorities; if we had so much free time, why didn't we shorten the release schedule?

The lesson we painfully learned was that a change effort should be as securely launched as possible, before there is too much attention drawn to it. To be sure, the time will come (and quite soon) when publicity will be the objective; raising the awareness of your users will be the goal of an entire phase (see Chapter 5). Also at some point you will require resources and funding for implementation just as you would for any project, and therefore you will have to seek and obtain the commitment of your management (see Chapter 4). Moreover, we are not suggesting massive paranoia; in your environment, an open policy on day 1 may be just right for your effort.

Another option you might consider is sharing your plans with a trusted individual, such as an employee, a peer or your boss. Obviously an employee or peer can be a great asset in terms of making progress while the change effort is still a part-time operation. Your boss can be invaluable in many ways. For example, he can begin subtly laying the groundwork for selling the productivity improvement to upper management. He will also be able to assist you by arranging time for you to keep the change process moving forward during these early days.

It is a fact that during these early phases of implementing change, the process can be compared to a small and fragile child. You must both protect and nurture your effort until its future is secure. Indeed, during the later stage of the life cycle (as we will discuss in Chapter 12), you will experience difficulties in the opposite direction, such as a need to control the process and prevent it from moving forward too quickly. However, in the beginning the main ingredients for progress and success will be your assessment and judgment of the situation, a nurturing and protective attitude, and most important your own commitment and even fervor.

SUMMARY

- Since data processing as a profession (as well as the individuals who practice it) has matured, we have begun to invest time and effort in improving productivity.
- Although the introduction of new technology is difficult, just as surely as there is a software development life cycle, so there exists a life cycle for implementing change.
- As an agent of change, the first activity in which you must engage is assessing your organization to ensure that the time is right to introduce a productivity improvement.
- Since you will be a critical success factor, it is imperative that you are committed and that you fully appreciate the tremendous significance of what is being undertaken.
- To be absolutely certain that the change you are implementing will substantially improve the lives of potential users, you must quantify the projected benefits.

2
Selecting the Candidate Products

The guiding star for you during this phase must be to set reasonable limits in terms of time and scope. We have all known people who have undertaken the responsibility for productivity tool selection and then disappeared for the next decade. Since no one deliberately sets out to make a career of tool selection, we must begin by identifying why this is a trap into which so many people stumble. The trap is very simply due to a phenomenon that we call "chasing the rainbow"; i.e., there is so much software and hardware currently available or under development that it is literally possible to search forever for the perfect tool.

The fact that there are so many choices is further complicated by one of the very personality traits that attracts us to data processing—our interest in and enjoyment of new technology. This predisposition on our parts enables us to experience an almost childlike joy in this phase. What lies immediately ahead are the tasks of discovering and exploring new tools or techniques, and then determining their applicability to your environment. You will also have the opportunity to meet and interact with many new people. All these activities and interactions will be quite intellectually stimulating. Moreover, since it may often seem that we are bombarding you with concerns, cautions, and hazards to avoid, it is reassuring to realize that there will actually be activities that will be enjoyable.

However it must be clear that not only are the possibilities virtually limitless, but also the process of selecting can be itself seductively fun. Therefore the critical success factor for this phase becomes the fundamental issue of setting your own limits. First of all, you must consciously separate selecting candidate products from the process of in-depth evaluation. The selection phase should include a market survey of what is currently available and culminate in selecting a few (no more than three or four) products that will be thoroughly evaluated in the next phase. This distinction is essential, because if you begin the selection process with an exhaustive critique of products, you will inevitably succumb to the "chasing the rainbow" syndrome.

To assist in the process of setting limits, we offer the following four axioms, which have proved invaluable to us:

1. To avoid premature and nonproductive attention to detail, keep your objective firmly in mind at all times; i.e., to perform a market survey of possible products.
2. Set a specific date by which time you will have made your selection.
3. Have a specific (not necessarily complex or detailed) procedure firmly in mind before you begin.
4. Have a very clear definition of what would be required in order for this tool to be effective.

SETTING THE DUE DATE

It may seem that setting your due date will be affected by many factors, such as the complexity and magnitude of the change, and whether or not you are still acting under your own initiative. However, we have implemented change in a wide variety of areas—from a new editor to automated software for the whole development process—and firmly believe that selection time cannot exceed two months. This may seem minimal to you, but don't forget this is a survey only, and does not include an in-depth evaluation of even one product.

Although it may seem that this time frame is arbitrarily brief, it is essential that you consider how quickly everything changes in data processing (people, technology, methods). Therefore, if the combined time for selection and evaluation exceeds three to four months, there is a high probability that your original assumptions and assessment will no longer be valid (see Figure 2–1).

Let me share with you an experience where we were thwarted in our attempt to implement change by a lack of timeliness. At that time, which was quite a few years ago, I worked for a dynamic boss who was not only enthusiastic but also technically astute. He was the type of individual with a steady stream of new ideas about a myriad of ways to apply the latest breakthroughs in our field to applications development. This was the data processing era, when microcomputers were just becoming viable in commercial data processing, and my boss began a self-initiated study of their applicability to our environment.

I was chosen as his fellow agent of change, and together we assessed our organization's needs, as well as the timing for this type of change. He shared and sold our concept to upper management, who supported our efforts. In fact, our study was well publicized internally and externally. In certain areas, the results were eagerly awaited. We proceeded through all the steps that will be outlined in

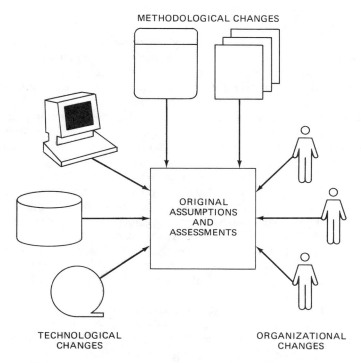

METHODOLOGICAL CHANGES

ORIGINAL
ASSUMPTIONS
AND
ASSESSMENTS

TECHNOLOGICAL
CHANGES

ORGANIZATIONAL
CHANGES

Figure 2–1 External change can adversely affect a change effort.

this chapter and made considerable progress quite rapidly. It is not at all difficult for me to remember the satisfaction and even pleasure I received from performing the tasks assigned by my boss. He not only exposed me to many new trade journals and magazines, but also to whole new areas of the computer field. He enabled me to gain confidence in my planning, technical, and interpersonal skills. We visited many different vendor sites as well as those of other customers. All in all, we had fun!

At last, we were putting together the final report, which included a detailed recommendation for strategic implementation of micros in key development projects. At that point we experienced difficulty with our new word processor creating some tables that were an attachment for our report. These difficulties delayed distribution by several weeks. During these two weeks, our department underwent a major reorganization and our group was moved to another department with different upper management. The new management considered microcomputers toys that had no place in our environment. We were not permitted to distribute even a draft version of our report!

I still have a copy of this study and I still believe that much of it was insightful and that the information would have been useful to many people. Moreover, if we had issued the report without the tables, it would have been just as valuable to every one of our potential readers. However, we lost sight of our major objective, unnecessarily delayed our due date, and thus were undone by time and politics. We are not advocating a sloppy job at any step of the way; but it's a fact that even if something is of the highest quality, it is useless if time and opportunity have passed. Of course, you are the one who chose the target area, and now you must be the one who will ultimately decide how much time to allow. The main point is to establish a cutoff time and then not to revise it.

Having examined the adverse effect of inadvertently changing the due date, let's examine a few of the factors that may seem to affect not only time allotted, but also approach taken for selection. The area you have targeted for change would seem to dictate the time and manner of your search. For example, looking for a new word processor is a whole different order of magnitude in complexity than finding a new life cycle methodology. Not only will the impact of a new word processor be minimal compared to a whole new methodology, but the products themselves will be substantially simpler to consider. On the other hand, there will certainly be a tremendous number of word processors available on the market compared to life cycle methodologies. You must allow enough time to perform a reasonable survey for even the most minimal change. Truly, the bottom line is that no matter what type of product you are searching for, the amount of time required or the approach taken will not substantially vary.

In Chapter 1 we discussed the pros and cons of acting solely on your own initiative versus enlisting management involvement from the beginning. During the selection phase, there is no compelling reason that should direct you to alter your decision in either direction. The guidelines discussed in the last chapter remain applicable; soliciting management support will be dictated by a combination of your unique situation, your organization, and your management. However, if your management is aware of your efforts or possibly even directing the process, a due date may well be predetermined. Moreover, it is highly probable that you will be given more time than we are recommending for this phase. If that is the case, exercise restraint, complete the survey within two months, and pleasantly surprise your management.

If you are given a mandate to compress the survey into less time, you should seriously examine the possibility of complying. If this does not appear to be a viable alternative, then you must present your management with a list of activities to be performed during this phase so that they can appreciate that you do indeed need more time. In the next section we will discuss the specific activities that comprise this phase. However, before we move to this topic, we need to recap some salient points about setting the due date:

- Due to the rapidly changing environment of data processing, time allotted for the selection phase should not exceed two months.
- The complexity of the product for which you are searching will not cause the amount of time to vary substantially.
- If you are acting under management directive and are given many months for the product search, you must still limit the time to two months.

Finally, whether you are working with your management or alone, you must establish a time frame to which you are truly committed (publicly or in your mind only).

PERFORMING THE MARKET SURVEY

Now that you have a target date, you must begin the concrete tasks of candidate product selection. These tasks are truly so simple and straightforward that they may seem at times almost childlike. The first thing you should do is gather as many trade journals as you can easily obtain. Don't visit every computer store in the state; approximately 8 to 10 major magazines or journals are more than sufficient for almost any product category. Next, you will spend no more than two or three days surveying the literature for products you will investigate.

You will want to keep track of all products that you consider. It does not matter if you dismiss a product as a possibility a mere five minutes after it was brought to your attention; you still need a record that it was considered. This record will be useful throughout the selection process; it should be kept (as well as the detailed product information) as a source of historical background information in the future, when people may have questions about the process you followed.

A number of years ago, I was the project manager for the development of a UNIX system. Not surprisingly, one of the significant issues we had to address and resolve was selection of a Data Base Management System (DBMS). Both during and after the market survey, we kept extensive (not necessarily formal) records of all the possibilities considered. This modest effort saved us a tremendous amount of time and energy many times during the development of the system. As it turned out, the DBMS we selected was not the most prevalent or even a popular choice. Therefore, as the project proceeded, many people questioned the wisdom of our choice. Once we were called upon (at very short notice) to provide our director with information about all the products considered, as well as the rationale for our selection. Many of the casual inquiries were satisfied by the fact that documentation of the selection and evaluation process existed. However, some of the requests, such as those from technical support and operations, resulted in people receiving valuable information. In any case, whether requests are motivated by politics or true need for information, you will never regret the minimal investment you make in keeping track of your market survey.

How you might record this information is up to you: The level of detail, as well as how formally you document this phase, is extremely flexible. If you are operating on your own and are pressed for time, a simple list that contains all products, vendor names, addresses, and phone numbers, in addition to reason for exclusion from or inclusion in the evaluation phase, should be sufficient. If months later (when your implementation is successfully proceeding), you are questioned about this phase, it will be viewed as a miracle that you kept any records of all.

On the other hand, if this is your full-time assignment, you will probably be expected to provide your management with a report at the end of this phase. The contents of the report as well as the format will vary from one organization to another. Some groups with which I have worked were satisfied with the information described above, while others required a matrix where the columns and rows were dictated by local conventions. Some PC-based products such as Lightyear support this process, and may even remove some of the subjectivity by allowing you to specify weighting factors to predetermined selection criteria.

THE VENDOR RELATIONSHIP

After you have selected some products that indicate promising features, you will spend a few days calling each vendor to request detailed product information. The importance of these phone calls to you as a change agent cannot be minimized, because this is the beginning of a very important and useful business relationship. After all, the vendor of the product you ultimately recommend will be supporting your efforts during the entire implementation of your productivity improvement.

But even though these phone calls are important, you should not be at all hesitant about contacting numerous salespeople, because the overwhelming majority of vendors will be extremely cooperative. Moreover, even though they may view you as a potential customer, most will not be overtly aggressive. If you should encounter difficulties with a vendor, this can only be viewed as useful information. For example, if a particular person with whom you are dealing is very uncooperative, you should consider that individual a representative of that vendor. Then when you are making your selection, you might wonder about the quality of support you will get after you purchase the product. (We will address this possibility in detail when we discuss the evaluation phase in the next chapter.)

On the other hand, you must ensure from the very first conversation that you also treat each vendor contact forthrightly and with respect. For example, you must make it very clear that you are performing an investigation only at this time. You want the salespeople with whom you will be dealing to understand clearly that you do not want to incur an expense at this point and that you are not interested in discussing contracts or licenses. You do, however, want price information included with the brochures they send you. There is absolutely no benefit or even need to act as though a major purchase is imminent when it is not. That you represent a potential customer will be evident to any responsive salesperson.

Actually, basic honesty between yourself and your vendor contacts is the only viable option in the long run. I had a friend who worked for a major corporation and was quite boastful of his prowess in the arena of vendor manipulation. He was taken out for many free lunches, provided with expedited service, and loaned products with no associated charge. These interactions proceeded until it became obvious that a purchase was not forthcoming. Approximately a year later, my friend had a different assignment in which it would have been quite beneficial to incorporate the vendor's product. Although he complained bitterly about the vendor's decline in responsiveness, it was no surprise to us that his phone calls were hardly ever returned.

Since you of course will conduct yourself in a reasonable manner, most people will respond accordingly, be very helpful, and soon swamp you with brochures and price lists. As soon as you have any information at all, you must begin analyzing the individual products in relationship to your organization's requirements. Remember, the goal is to narrow the products down to a few possibilities that someone will evaluate in detail. Moreover, you must by this time have the requirements firmly determined.

Before we proceed with requirement formation, let's summarize the steps you have taken thus far:

1. A date has been set that will end with the selection of candidate products.
2. You have surveyed the market for available products.
3. Your survey has been recorded for historical reference.
4. You have contacted the vendors of the products.
5. Detailed information, including prices, is on the way.

Note how much has been accomplished, and yet you are only on week 2 of the time allotted (see timeline in Figure 2–2). This fact may give some credence and even comfort to the thought of allowing only one to two months for this phase.

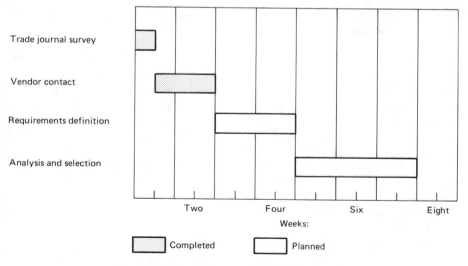

Figure 2–2   Typical time required for selection phase.

DEFINING THE REQUIREMENTS

It is essential that you perform this step at this juncture: The chances of any product having every feature that is on your requirement list is extremely slim; however, if you do not know precisely what you want, an undesirable scenario may unfold. As you examine products and find some that are quite good, you may unconsciously keep expanding the hazy picture of what you want. Indeed, this scenario is a classic case of the "chasing the rainbow" syndrome described at the beginning of the chapter.

In order to understand how very easy it is to slip into this syndrome, let's reflect on the following story. Imagine you are selecting a new data base management system (DBMS) for your department. You have eagerly accepted (or initiated) this challenge and have thoroughly enjoyed your market survey. During your analysis of the product literature you find a very promising DBMS; it is relational, compatible with your current hardware/software environment, and reasonably priced. You should now proceed to the next phase for an in-depth evaluation; but when you think about it, you wish that the DBMS supported a screen generator. So you search further by analyzing the product literature again, or you may even resurvey the market. Eventually you find another product that seems to have all the qualifications of the first one, including the screen generator. However, instead of proceeding with an in-depth evaluation, you start looking for a product with an on-line help facility.

It is not hard to believe that you can easily fall into this trap; nor is it hard to imagine that you will never find a product that fulfills your need (which is constantly expanding), and that you might indeed search forever (see Figure 2–3). On the other hand, if you had clearly defined your requirements, you could have rapidly compared these requirements to each product as you received detailed information about it.

In the ideal situation, requirements would have already been analyzed and documented by you or others, and this situation is actually not as unlikely as it might seem. I know that this can happen because when we implemented a CASE tool, that was exactly the situation. For a variety of reasons, very difficult times had come to our organization, and morale was very low. Upper management had commissioned a task force of middle managers to assess the situation and come up with a recommendation for relief. They thoroughly evaluated all the circumstances and clearly identified a need for analyst support to improve the following phases of the software development life cycle: user requirements, system definition, and logical design. A group of analysts was chartered to develop and document the requirements for a new system that one of the project teams would then develop.

The requirements document had been completed, but due to funding considerations, development of a new system was not a possibility. A year later, when we were searching for a CASE tool, my boss (who had been one of the middle managers on the task force) utilized this document during the process that resulted

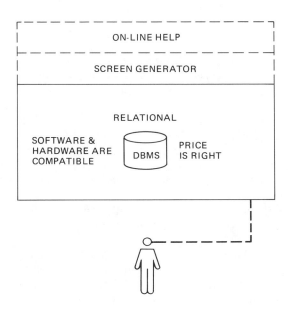

Figure 2–3 Chasing the rainbow.

in our selection of Excelerator. There is, of course, an obvious moral to this story: Neither you nor other change agents may have been part of any effort that resulted in requirements being developed. However, it may well be worth investing a small amount of time investigating the possible existence of any remotely related material. As an agent of change you will be constantly racing against time, and thus there is absolutely no advantage in redoing any work already completed.

If you are not so lucky, then you need to document a set of well-developed requirements before you proceed with the analysis of the product literature. It is not at all necessary that this document be a formal one, particularly if you are operating on your own. Of course, if your management is involved, they may have some very definite requests that you will have to satisfy. In any case, bear in mind your time constraints and by all means keep it as simple as possible. We have employed a technique as primitive as listing user requirements and then organizing them into bulleted items by category. The critical aspects of this activity were to determine clearly in our own minds what was required, document this information (formally or informally), and then utilize the document as a reference during the analysis.

When you are documenting the requirements and analyzing each product, keep the following three points firmly in mind:

- Who your users are and how this product will improve their work lives
- Never getting stuck on a particularly snazzy product
- Ensuring that the benefits are not obscure

EMPLOYING EMPATHY

The first objective is to determine what will truly benefit your users. You do not ever want to introduce a management method to control, which becomes a burden to them, but rather a product that will truly add something to the work process. This determination is a critical success factor, because if you do not truly add value, then you will never gain the acceptance of your users. After all, they are intelligent professionals who are so busy they are already stretched to their collective limits. Thus although it is safe to assume that none of us would ever intentionally select a product that does not really benefit, it is still quite possible that we might inadvertently do so. The art of ensuring that this is not the case relies heavily on employing the skill of empathy.

Empathy is defined as identification with and understanding of another's situation, feelings, and motives, and is really an ability to step back and imagine yourself in the place of another person. For example, suppose you are searching for a project control and tracking tool. The average project manager is overworked and behind schedule, as you can probably quite vividly remember from your own recent experiences. When you were not dealing with dissatisfied users, you were probably explaining to your management why you were behind schedule, and trying to keep the programming staff on the right track.

As a change agent, you have just found a fantastic tool that will keep track of every activity and can generate graphs and reports by person or by day or by activity. However, the only way to ensure accuracy is for the project manager to personally spend a half-hour every day inputting data. Can you really imagine a positive reaction from your potential and exceptionally busy users? It might be a different story if we were talking about a startup problem. In that case, there would be some initial obstacles to overcome, but you could imagine yourself (and thus your users) eventually accepting and even welcoming such a product. Moreover, it is highly likely that the project managers would welcome and appreciate a tool that does a little less, but requires no additional effort from them.

In general, people are very busy, and they don't view anything new as positive—especially if it is going to require considerable training initially and then require them to perform extra job functions. You may not have to convince anyone at this stage except yourself, but if you are going to be successful at implementing change, you will have to convince many people. Just imagine yourself doing their jobs, and avoid anything that might add extra and annoying steps to their already hectic days.

AVOID RAZZLE DAZZLE

You also must avoid selecting slick, exotic products. Never forget that due to our technical backgrounds and propensity to leading edge products, we are quite susceptible to marketing hype. Moreover, it will appear (and rightly so) that razzle dazzle will substantially assist us when we are presenting the tool, but may well be counterproductive during and/or after actual implementation. Suppose you found a word processor that operates very impressively on a color monitor; and you even have the option of selecting among shades of green, red, etc. Furthermore, when you bring up this word processor, it generates a picture of a user and then a terminal. The user walks over to the terminal, turns it around to face you, and the product's logo leaps out and covers the screen in brilliant color. This product would capture the attention of even the most jaded and cynical. Images of yourself demonstrating this tool to your director or even the vice president fill your mind. Months pass, and you are now dealing with some harsh realities. It turns out only 10% of your users have color monitors. Moreover, everyone, including yourself, is fed up with the user, the terminal, and the leaping logo, which takes up a considerable amount of time whenever you want to use the product. This is a striking example of the seduction described at the beginning of the chapter. You must never let go of your practicality when you are examining potential products, because you as well as your users will have to live with your choices for a long, long time.

THE RIGHT PRODUCT FOR THE RIGHT ORGANIZATION

One final caution we might offer is that you must also ensure that the benefits of the selected products will be reasonably obvious to the people in your organization. In Chapter 1 we described several methods for assessing your organization. Therefore, you have surely and correctly selected a target area where there is a real need for improvement and where the gains will be substantial. However, if you find a virtually perfect product, but to most people none of its benefits are recognizable or it requires years to realize the benefit, you will find it almost impossible to convince your users and management.

Timeliness of your implementation is critical and will be discussed thoroughly in Chapter 8. But the other aspect of enabling your users and management to perceive the benefits is related to the modality of your organization. Every department (and to certain extent even an individual work group) very rapidly develops its own general pattern of operations. There are unspoken sentiments that affect most daily interactions and that include a set of collective priorities. For example, it may be clear to you the business planning methodology that you have selected will substantially improve the quality of the systems being developed by your organization. However, it is a fact that these people have a very informal approach to the software development life cycle; i.e., they really only want to code programs. The current mode of operation here barely addresses design, and thus you can be sure there will be zero interest in planning.

The benefits of even the most perfect business planning methodology would be virtually impossible for this group to comprehend. Furthermore, if by some miracle you were able to begin implementation of this methodology, you would initially be changing the very beginning of the project's life cycle. Since these people are into the code, it will take months or even years to realize some concrete results to which they can relate. Because this organization is into instant gratification you would have a higher chance of success here with a programmer productivity tool, such as a code generator. It is crucial to realize and accept that in addition to providing a product that truly adds benefit, your users and management must also be in a position to appreciate this benefit.

The selection phase is fraught with many potential and even seductive pitfalls into which a change agent can stumble and remain for a very long time. This is probably more true for this phase than many others due to the combination of tasks involved and our predisposition toward technology. However, you are now armed not only with a well marked trail to follow, but also which attractive but dangerous paths to avoid. Therefore you can confidently enjoy the aspects of product selection that are so attractive without being seduced into remaining there forever.

SUMMARY

- To ensure successful completion of this phase, you must limit both the time and the scope of your market survey.
- Although the products for which you are searching may vary considerably in complexity, the time allotted should not exceed two months.
- During this phase you will set the tone of your vendor relationships. This is very important because you will be dealing with one of them for the entire change process.
- Before selecting any product, you must clearly define the requirements so that you do not risk the possibility of searching forever for the perfect product.
- To assist you in requirement formation, use empathy, avoid razzle dazzle, and base your selection on the modality of your organization.

3

Evaluating the Products

The primary critical success factor during the evaluation phase is who evaluates the product. Not only is it essential to ensure a thorough and realistic appraisal, but it will also be of paramount importance for credibility during the entire implementation.

With this thought in mind, let's examine a list of skills and experience that we recommend for the evaluator:

1. Recent and extensive experience in the area being targeted for change
2. Progressive rather than reactionary personality
3. Practical and business orientation, as well as a technical background
4. Highly developed analytical skills

WHO PERFORMS THE EVALUATION?

The first item on the list is the key to a successful evaluation. In many instances, selection as well as evaluation is performed by a centralized support group. This group might be in charge of corporate standards, quality assurance, technical support, or even training. It is the firm conviction of most project managers as well as programmers and end users that this is a misplaced responsibility. It is impossible for anyone to judge the added value of any product except the people who will be doing the job and actually utilizing the tools or techniques. These may seem like strong statements, but experience certainly bears out their veracity.

For example, when we selected and evaluated Excelerator, we were part of a project team that maintained and enhanced an order processing system. Moreover, we had during the previous few years worked on this system from an analyst /user perspective as well as in the actual development of some of its subsystems. Therefore, we were uniquely qualified to determine the applicability of an automated tool for the people who participated in all aspects of the project team. Indeed, our grass roots beginnings prevented the resentment that usually accompanies recommendations issued by centralized groups. All the facts and figures in our business case were based on specific occurrences in the development life cycle of this system. Both management and workers acknowledged and accepted the fact that our evaluation was based on an accurate and complete understanding of the jobs that were being performed.

On the other hand, we are not trying to say that centralized groups do not have a very important part to play in terms of coordination. They are crucial in ensuring that individual departments are not evolving incompatibly in areas where there may be a need in the future to share detailed information. Imagine two different applications groups that are developing separate and distinct systems (A and B). They are each evolving a standard employee id; however, system A is using social security number and system B is using login id. Suppose that in the future these systems will interface and pass employee data to each other. At that point, both development groups will have a substantial and perhaps on-going problem that will certainly affect productivity.

This problem might have been averted if there had been involvement by a centralized group responsible for long-range strategic planning. The planning group would have been in a position to foresee the interface and the related problems. This information would have been shared with the two development groups, a common employee id could have been used, and the two groups would have been as productive over time as they were initially. Figure 3–1 provides a graphic illustration of the future interfaces between systems A and B with and without centralized support group involvement.

Centralized groups also have a role to play by adding technological expertise—by ensuring that selected products can be readily incorporated into the existing software/hardware environment. For example, suppose you completed a very favorable evaluation of a new editor for the minicomputer environment that already exists in your company. You predict that successful implementation (within 18 months) will increase on-line usage by 40%. An additional factor that must be considered in this case is the effect of this increase on the network. Thus, you will need to involve technical support in your evaluation. However, it is also obvious that although technical support is crucial for an accurate evaluation, these experts really are not in a favorable position to tell applications developers what editor to use. The point being made here is that each group has a role to play, and it is really just a question of which one is in the best position to address each issue most effectively.

Another factor that should be considered is the personality type of the evaluator; this relates to items two, three, and four on the list. You would certain-

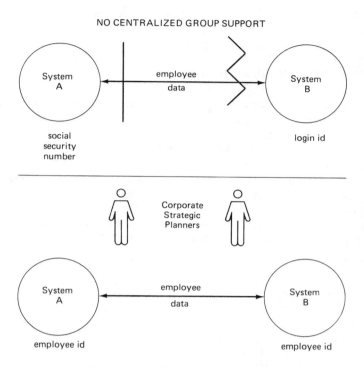

Figure 3–1 Role of centralized groups.

ly not ask the most negative person in your group (the one who doesn't ever change the orientation of his stapler on his desk) to evaluate a new way of performing his job. You want to choose an individual who has demonstrated open-mindedness. However, you also want to avoid the "whiz kid" syndrome—the programmer who is not only always experimenting with something new, but is always one step beyond the leading edge of technology. What you do need is a person who in addition to being a competent analyst and technician is level-headed enough to determine practical applications for the product.

This may seem a bit vague; however, it is actually very easy to pick the required person from your group (or indeed maybe it is yourself). Remember the last time you introduced your group to something new? Perhaps you were showing them a new personal computer recently acquired for your project team. There might have been one person who wondered aloud why we would bother with this when we all already had terminals that connected to a mainframe in Indiana; this is the negative, resistant to change personality. There also might have been one inquisitive sort who asked you exactly what was happening to the floppy diskette when you formatted it; this is the techy type who may well get lost in the details. But there also might have been someone who observed how much easier it might be to document the next logical design using the PC's word processor; this is the person you want. She is thinking of practical applications before she has even had a chance to touch finger to keyboard.

STRUCTURING THE EVALUATION

Now that you have someone who is ready to evaluate the products, you must work out a structure for a trial of each candidate. This trial must provide a reasonable test of each product's capabilities and limitations. You will need to specify individual activities, the people who will be responsible, and time frames. The same principles that dictated the necessity of limiting time and scope in the selection phase (see Chapter 2) are equally applicable during the evaluation. Remember that this is not a stress test; you only need to be reasonably sure that the product will substantially improve things, not that it is perfect. Do not be concerned with preparing a formal schedule; you just need to document all the steps (see Figure 3–2) and dependencies for your own use during this phase.

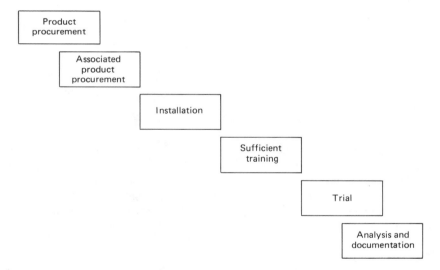

Figure 3–2 Steps of the evaluation phase.

Of course, the specific details of the steps may vary from product to product, but it is clear that they address areas you must consider including in the activities of your trial. Therefore, you can use the following list as a basis to be customized to your individual situation:

1. Procurement of products to be evaluated
2. Procurement of any associated hardware or software
3. Installation of all products and associated hardware/software

4. Sufficient training to judge the products

5. Utilization of products in real-life situation or a simulated trial

6. Analysis of the results and documentation of the entire evaluation process

PRODUCT PROCUREMENT AND TRAINING

The first step, procuring the products, will drive your schedule and therefore must be given primary consideration. Moreover, this process will be affected by many factors, such as the price of the products and your own budget. The money available to you is also directly related to the degree to which your management is aware of and supports your effort. If you are acting under the direction of upper management and are part of a large organization that is already committed to productivity improvement, you will probably be able to spend quite a bit of money. In this case, the determining factor will be the price of each individual product. If the tools operate on a PC, they will probably be relatively inexpensive, and you may be able to purchase several of the most promising candidates. If the tools are meant to be part of a more complex computer environment, you may be able to arrange a monthly lease. Some vendors will then deduct the rental money from the price, if you finally purchase the product. On the other hand, if you are operating largely on your own or are part of a small organization or your budget is severely limited, there are still several options available to you.

The first possible source you will want to explore is the vendor of the products. Vendors can be invaluable during this phase, and any assistance they offer should be seriously considered. I have known people who refuse to even talk to vendor representatives and I have wondered why they have adopted this attitude. Perhaps they fear they will be subjected to nothing but marketing hype or they are uncomfortable because they are too proud to ask for and receive help. But whatever is the reason, this is foolish; the vendor can be your best ally at this point.

Even if the vendor turns out to be a very unpleasant person, as we mentioned in the previous chapter, this information should be included in the evaluation. If this company is difficult to deal with before the sale, the level of support will only worsen afterward. Years ago we bought a piece of hardware from a very unpleasant salesman. He was uncooperative and rude, even when we were trying to deal with him for the purpose of spending thousands of dollars. Since no other product even began to match the capabilities of his, we proceeded with the purchase, and I can honestly say that the product worked out quite well in our environment. However, every interaction we had with his company was unpleasant: training was poor, the hotline was virtually nonexistent, even delivery and billing were complicated by errors on the vendor's part.

The majority of vendors are quite helpful and will arrange many services that do not cost anything. They can almost always arrange demonstrations (nearby or on-site) for you and your peers or management. You may also request the names of other customers who have purchased the products. You should talk to several of these people and if possible visit them to see how they are using the tools. Some vendors will loan the tools for a nominal fee or even without charge if you explain that you are doing an evaluation and will guarantee their safe return within a specified amount of time. When we were looking at project control and tracking tools, we borrowed a copy of Project Workbench (PW) from the vendor for 60 days at no charge. We did have to sign an agreement stating our purpose and promising not to copy anything (software or documentation). Also included in the terms of the agreement was our responsibility to return everything undamaged within 60 days (which was more than enough time to evaluate the product).

Before we move to the next step of this phase, let's summarize the various methods for product procurement that we have described:

1. Purchase one or more candidates if price and budget permit.
2. Lease one or more candidates if price and budget permit.
3. Talk to and/or visit other customers who are already utilizing the products.
4. Solicit and accept all vendor support, such as in-depth demonstrations and loan of products.

The next step, procurement of associated hardware or software, will for the most part follow the same rules as procurement of the products themselves. Certainly this will also drive the schedule and thus must be addressed early in the process. It is also directly related to price and budget. We have listed it separately because it is sometimes overlooked in the beginning of this phase, and since other steps are dependent upon this one, much valuable time can be lost.

There is an additional reason to keep associated products separate that is related to the budget. If the products can be utilized for activities and/or projects that extend beyond your trial and evaluation, their cost should not be linked to your immediate effort. One PC product we evaluated required a mouse, and we were able to purchase this without associating the cost to our evaluation because its usefulness was not bounded by our trial. The expenditure was therefore charged against a more general budget, one associated with graphics we used for training, presentations, etc.

Step three, installation, should not be underestimated even if you are dealing with a very modest PC-based product. After all, you may be in an environment where none of your associates has ever used a PC before, or perhaps this product will be fundamentally incompatible with every other package already installed on the PC. None of these events is insurmountable, but they could happen; if they do, they will take up some of your valuable allotted evaluation time, so you must be prepared (at least in terms of schedule).

If this is a mainframe product, you may have to deal with centralized support groups such as operations or technical support. Then you have additional layers of complexity to consider. These factors will definitely affect your schedule, and thus you must carefully weigh the time required versus the benefits of performing the trial at your site. Moreover, if your trial will involve any other organizations, your entire effort must already be public knowledge and approved by upper management.

If you do determine that the magnitude (expense, scope, etc.) of the productivity improvement warrants an on-site trial and your effort has already been legitimatized, then you are the best judge of it. However, some of the alternatives can be quite acceptable and thus should also be given careful thought. When we performed an evaluation for our microcomputer study (see previous chapter), we relied heavily on in-depth demonstrations at vendor locations. For some of the products, we also visited other organizations within our corporation. The quality and depth of information we gathered through these channels was more than sufficient, given the time and scope of our study.

You do want to avoid unnecessarily complicating the situation. If you need an on-site trial, by all means have one. However, if this would drag out the evaluation another 6 months, seriously consider whether the product warrants this. Is it possible that your objectives could really be met by visiting other sites? The main point (of which you must never lose sight) is that you must identify specific and realistic activities, recognize dependencies, and produce a reasonable schedule that accurately reflects this.

You will notice that the fourth step of this phase, which deals with training, uses the word *sufficient*. This is an important point to bear in mind; you do not have to become an acknowledged expert on the tool you are judging. You do, however, need to have enough understanding of the product to determine the extent to which it will add benefit to how you are currently performing your job. Most products are packaged with some type of tutorial, including on-line exercises, and this may be enough training for you and your group to evaluate the tool properly. If you do require more instruction, this is another area where the vendor may be able to help. Many vendors will send representatives to your site for a day to help get your people accustomed to their product quickly. We even had the experience when we were looking at business planning tools of a vendor who insisted on giving us a one-day workshop so we would be truly able to evaluate his product.

THE ACTUAL TRIAL

In terms of actually testing the product (the fifth step), the optimal scenario would be to use the tool or technique in a real situation. For example, you have a prototyping tool and you are at the point in the project life cycle where you are about to gather, analyze, and finalize user requirements. However, since in real life you are usually not that fortunate, you might consider simulation as an alternative. In the case of the prototyping tool, you could employ role playing; one staff member could act as a user, another as an analyst, and they could simulate the requirements phase of development.

In either case, as preparation for the actual trial you should list specific activities that will be performed before, during, and after its execution. Some of these activities will correspond directly to the steps of the phase and will be quite universal. However, the activities performed during the actual trial execution will be unique to each candidate product. They should be based on the requirements (gathered and documented in the selection phase), the advertised capabilities of the tools (from the detailed product information), as well as the job functions typically performed in the area being targeted for change.

To provide an example of a trial, let's expand upon the prototyping scenario that was mentioned above. Suppose the requirements specified (among other things) that we are looking for a microcomputer-based product for under $5,000 which can readily be incorporated into our current environment. Let's also suppose the leading candidate product claims to produce the COBOL data division based on screens that are prototyped. Moreover, you have also selected customer credit check as the function that will be prototyped, either because it is a real user requirement or because this is the user need being simulated. In this situation, the following list of activities and time frames might comprise

Activity	Time Allotted
1. Purchase one copy of tool	1/2 day
2. Install package on local microcomputer	2 days
3. Take on-line tutorial and read documentation	3 days
4. Receive instruction from vendor	1 day
5. Analyze existing information on customer credit check function	1 day
6. Load data element definitions into tool's dictionary facility	2 days
7. Paint screens utilizing the tool	2 days
8. Load sample data using tool's database manager	2 days
9. Prototyping session	1 day
10. Generate COBOL data division	1/2 day
11. Analysis and documentation	5 days

In this example, we covered the more general steps of procurement, installation, training, and analysis, as well as addressing specific selection requirements, the product's advertised capabilities, and job functions performed in real life (see Figure 3–3). When you prepare your activity list, you may want to note dependencies and specify who is responsible for each item. However, make sure you don't get too involved in chart creation; keep it simple. You will, of course, need to adapt it to your own style and the dictates of the area in which you are implementing change.

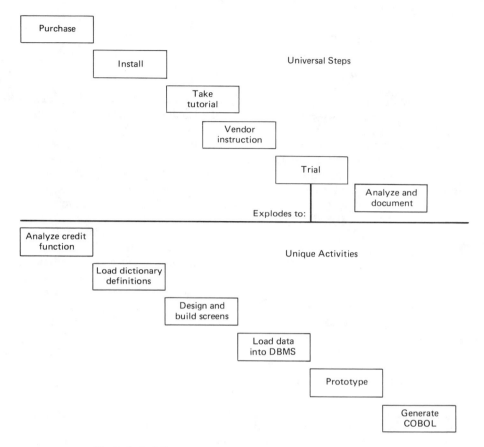

Figure 3–3   Microcomputer prototyping tool product evaluation.

ANALYZE AND DOCUMENT

Note that activity item 11 (analysis and documentation) addresses the last step (number 6) in this phase: analyze all the information and document the entire process. Below you will find some sections that you might want to include in your documentation:

1. Executive overview
2. Description of trial
3. Detailed evaluation of products
4. Projected benefits
5. Conclusion

Appendices

A. Requirements from selection phase
B. Schedule and activity list from trial
C. Samples produced utilizing the products

In the last few pages of this chapter, we will take each section individually and discuss its importance and format. We will also describe the types of information that might be included, as well as additional techniques for gathering and analyzing this information. Please note that the contents and format of appendices A and B have already been discussed in this chapter and the previous one. Appendix C is quite straightforward; e.g., if the product is a DBMS, include the database definition and structure, as well as some sample record layouts.

The executive overview should include a brief statement of purpose—exactly what area is being targeted for change and why it was chosen. You might also want to share (on a high level) the scope of your selection and evaluation. It is also a good idea to provide a very brief description of each product. Section two will contain a brief description of the trial, as well as any limitations that arose. For example, you may not have been able to complete a particular activity that was originally scheduled. If you were unable to have an on-site trial of any products, you might want to explain how you proceeded. This will enable people to understand how you obtained all the information required to evaluate the products properly.

THE DETAILED EVALUATION

The detailed evaluation of products section will have specific criteria by which you are comparing the products and should also include the pros and cons of each one. The criteria by which you are judging the tools will, of course, vary depending on type of product. However, there are certain constants we believe should always be included:

1. Availability
2. Support
3. Training
4. Documentation
5. Ease of use
6. Compatibility

The first criterion that you must address is availability, and it is a very important one. Is the product available for purchase right now, or is it still under development? In general, products that have not been around for a while should be avoided. You cannot build an implementation plan around dates that have been promised by vendors. You are a project manager and are fully aware that no matter how good the intentions, target dates can be missed. One sure way to lose credibility (both with upper management and your users) is to be unable to proceed (at any phase of the implementation) because the product is still unavailable.

SEEK INPUT FROM OTHERS

In addition, if the product has been around for a while, there will be a higher likelihood that the support, training, and documentation (the next three criteria on our list) will be mature and robust. Whether or not these products have been around a while or not, you should make a serious attempt to speak to several other customers. They can provide a wealth of information on these three criteria as well as the next one, ease of use. You would like to know how long they have been using the product, as well as how extensively they are using it and if it has become an integral part of their operation. The following list of questions can be used as the basis of your conversations with these people:

1. How long have you been using this tool?
2. How many copies do you have of it?
3. How many users are supported by these copies?
4. What other tools did you compare it to?
5. What is your impression of the vendor?
6. How have you found the on-going level of support, documentation, and training?
7. Were your users already knowledgeable about any associated methodologies or techniques?
8. If not, how did that affect your implementation?
9. If you follow a formal development life cycle, has this tool and your use of it become part of that process?
10. Has the quality and/or timeliness of your system development improved?
11. Have you determined how much money has actually been saved by this productivity tool?
12. If you had it to do over, would you purchase this tool?

The questions on this list are very general, and you should augment them with questions that are relevant to the tools you are evaluating, your organization, and the applications that you foresee.

You can also capitalize on the experiences of yourself and your group during the selection and evaluation phases. You might want to ask yourself and your staff questions along the lines of the following:

1. How helpful was the vendor?

2. How helpful was the hotline?
3. Was the product literature in any way misleading?
4. How clear was the reference guide?
5. Was the tutorial hard or easy to follow?
6. Was the tutorial truly informative or was it largely comprised of busywork?
7. Is the product relatively easy to use?
8. Is it sophisticated enough to support many of the functions you are planning to mechanize?
9. Was it easy to get comfortable with?
10. Did you still experience considerable frustration even after the one day training session?
11. Are you disappointed with the product, or do you still feel optimistic about its benefits as well as the ease of incorporating it into your organization?

These questions may seem somewhat subjective, but you will have the opportunity to discuss them with other customers and your staff. Furthermore, you will thoroughly analyze your own impressions, and then you should have no trouble making a sound assessment of each candidate.

The final criterion, compatibility, verges on a philosophical view of the products. You want to ensure that they will not be fundamentally alien to the people who will be using them. For example, if your organization has a formal procedure that everyone follows for release planning and scheduling, you do not want to introduce a tool that would require everyone to follow a totally different procedure. What you want is a tool that enhances the tools, techniques, and procedures that already exist and can be gradually phased into the process.

We have come to the end of our discussion about the detailed evaluation of products, and we have attempted to provide some guidelines for information gathering and analysis. A final piece of advice is that it is a good idea at the end of this section to recommend one of the products and provide a rationale that will then be supported by the next section (projected benefits).

THE BUSINESS CASE

The projected benefits section is where you will include your business case. The quantification of projected benefits that you prepared as part of Assessing the Need (see Chapter 1) can serve as a basis for this. Review your original estimates and if necessary recalculate your projections based on new information you may have received. Since you now have precise price information, you can actually figure out the payback period—the time required to balance the expenditure with the savings. In our example (see Chapter 1), we estimated the following savings by employing a system test tool:

Projected savings is $60,000 per year
The price of the tool is $25,000 per copy
and we are recommending purchasing   3 copies

Thus our expenditure on software would be:

$$3 \times \$25,000 = \$75,000$$

We do not need any additional hardware
We do need to train each involved member of programming staff (MPS)

Cost of training is $5,000 per person

Thus our expenditure on training would be:

$$3 \times \$5,000 = \$15,000$$

Therefore our total cost would be:

Software		Hardware		Training		Total
$75,000	+	0	+	$15,000	=	$90,000

Since we project a savings of $60,000 per year, we can project that the payback period would be:

$$\$90,000/\$60,000 = 1.5 \text{ years}$$

In your business case, you would probably also want to describe any intangible savings you can foresee. In the scenario we depicted here, the intangibles might include transferring one of the senior MPS to a new applications development project. This type of people movement not only affords career opportunities for the individual, but also ensures that at least one member of the development group understands the purpose and mission of system test.

When you are preparing this business case, you might check to see if your organization has any standard format or document structure which you should follow. If not, consider the following as a checklist of topics that might be included in one format or another:

- An introduction that contains a brief paragraph or two explaining what is being mechanized
- A description (with dollar figures) of the current environment, including wage and nonwage expenses
- A description (with dollar figures) of the projected environment, including wage and nonwage expenses

- Projected benefits including intangibles

The last section of the evaluation document will be the conclusion. This may be the only section that is read by upper management, so it must be concise, to the point, and clear. Restate (briefly) purpose and scope, and then make your recommendations based on section three, detailed evaluation of products, and section four, projected benefits. You might want to refer to a few particularly significant facts from those sections. If there are any viable alternatives to your recommendation, briefly state them; if not, state that also. Try to confine this section to one page, and make the main points in the opening and closing sentences.

Let's review the last step of the evaluation phase via the graphic relationships depicted in Figure 3–4.

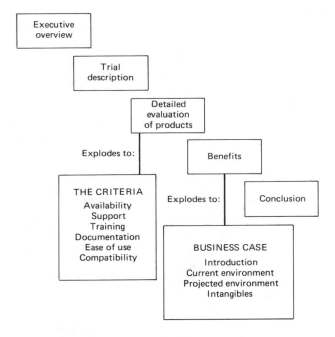

Figure 3–4 The evaluation document.

A FINAL THOUGHT

Now it is time for us to offer one final possibility for you to consider. It could happen that your experience thus far will lead you to conclude that the best path to follow is that of abandoning this productivity improvement at this time. Maybe there are no robust tools or techniques that are fully developed and available for purchase. Do not hesitate to recommend delay; your trial, detailed evaluation, and business case will support not only the delay, but the possibility of revisiting this area for productivity improvement in a year or even six months. There is no reason to be discouraged; you have already justified this productivity improvement via economic projections. All you have to do now is wait and technology will catch up with you. Moreover, you never want to proceed on a crusade when you are no longer a believer. As an agent of change, your own conviction is a critical success factor.

However, delay will not be the typical result at the end of the evaluation phase. In most cases, you will now have the tool or technique selected, evaluated, and the entire process documented, including a business case to justify proceeding. Furthermore, all this has been accomplished in a short time period, and thus it is highly unlikely that any of your original assumptions would have been even slightly affected by changing circumstances.

SUMMARY

- One of the critical success factors of this phase is who does the evaluation. Evaluators should be open-minded, practical people who are currently performing the job functions you are trying to automate.
- Organize this phase by developing and utilizing a list of activities that includes a schedule and people responsible for each item.
- You are working within a tight time frame, so keep the activities realistic and don't forget dependencies.
- Utilize all sources of information and help, including other customers or the vendor, who may well be your best resource during this phase.
- Analyze and document the entire process in the evaluation report, which will contain, among other sections, a business case and the requirements stated in the selection phase.
- Keep an open mind and base your recommendations on all factors, even if the conclusion is not what you expected.

4

Presenting the Product to Upper Management

In this phase, based upon the activities in which you will be involved, you may think you have been transferred to marketing. Make no mistake about it—this is a sales job! Furthermore, you will give a different type of sales pitch to different groups (upper management or users). Yet each sales pitch will have the same basic philosophy; you will always employ a soft sell.

The reason you have to take on this role has to do with the fact that during implementation, you will be effecting a cultural change. We discussed this aspect of the process in Chapter 1 when we discussed your own commitment. Now, however, we will get to the heart of the matter, which is simple and perhaps obvious: People naturally resist change. The overwhelming majority of us are quite comfortable with the way things are and do not see any reason to change.

OVERCOMING RESISTANCE

In fact, sometimes data processing people are particularly adverse to change. One explanation for this apparent contradiction relates directly to the nature of their work. Anyone who has ever developed and maintained systems understands the complexity of introducing change to software. Invariably, whenever a change (either to fix a problem or to enhance the system) is introduced, numerous problems crop up in other seemingly unrelated parts of the system. This phenomenon results not only in a reluctance to change software, but in a more generalized tendency to maintain the status quo procedurally or organizationally. Thus, in addition to being overworked and behind schedule, data processing people are also conservative.

We once had an extremely talented programmer in our group. He was an expert on the internals of the UNIX operating system, the type who proposed modifying the kernel (part of the operating system) for every system we developed. Every day he had a dozen suggestions, ranging from ways to optimize each program's performance to innovative methods that allowed user flexibility. But in relationship to his own habits of developing software, he was extremely rigid. For example, one portion of the system was PC-based and was to be developed using GWBASIC in an MS-DOS environment. The PCs, with which we were provided, already had the MS-DOS editor installed. Now our guru, who was responsible for this development effort, was accustomed to the UNIX VI editor. It was inconceivable that someone as bright as he would have required more than an hour to master the miracles of any editor. However, he spent almost an entire work day phoning all his friends until he succeeded in locating VI software for the PC!

What we have is the simple and obvious truth that it is difficult to implement productivity improvements because of human resistance. But it is not so simple—nor is it obvious—how to overcome this resistance. You and your group are few in number and yet you will be trying to modify the daily work habits of many (possibly even several hundred) individuals. It is no wonder that many brave souls have faltered in the face of this task. I have even heard people speculate that this is one reason so many crusaders remain in the selection and evaluation phases so long; it is certainly easier, and safer politically. However, you should not be unduly apprehensive, because in fact you have already moved safely through and past those phases. Moreover, formidable as it may seem at the outset, this cultural change has been effected successfully, and you will be provided with techniques to follow and suggestions about what to avoid, just as you were in the first three phases. In fact, the remaining chapters of the book deal with the step-by-step procedures that change agents can follow during the dramatic but gradual process of successfully implementing change.

Before we proceed with the presentation phase, let's do a quick check of all the assets available to you in the role of salesperson:

1. You have thoroughly analyzed your organization and its need for productivity improvement, as well as its readiness to accept change.

2. You have looked within yourself and realistically appraised your own commitment and willingness to take risk.

3. You have carefully selected the target area for change and quantified the projected benefits.

4. You have clearly stated the requirements of the productivity tool and/or technique.

5. You have surveyed the market and have detailed information about many products.

6. You have selected a few candidate products to be evaluated in detail.

7. You have performed a trial of each product that includes a reasonable test of the requirements, as well as each product's advertised capabilities.

8. You have talked to other customers and have analyzed their experiences as well as your own.
9. Based on all these factors and all the information, you have reached a sound conclusion and come up with a recommendation.
10. You have documented the entire process in an evaluation report that includes a business case, the requirements, and the recommendation.

You can now feel quite confident about communicating your plans for improving productivity in the target area. You have acquired substantial information, gained considerable experience with the product, and will be able to share this knowledge with others.

THE IMPORTANCE OF MANAGEMENT COMMITMENT

The first group you will want to approach is upper management, because this is the point in the implementation beyond which you cannot proceed without their consent. Moreover, if you already have this consent, a sales job is still in order. After all, there are varying degrees of support, and what is required is a high degree of commitment. Exactly why you need this commitment will be explained here, but first let's consider why we are placing such emphasis on this point at this particular time.

Up till now, everything you have done has involved only yourself, your group, and possibly your boss. Given the nature of what you were trying to accomplish, that was appropriate. In a certain sense, the first three phases were preliminary, and the time for you and a few others to prepare yourselves with facts, figures, and experience was essential. However, now you are entering the main phases of the change process. The first step involves raising the awareness of your department in connection with the product of choice. Obviously, this cannot be accomplished while your endeavors remain secret. Moreover, not only do you want your crusade to become public knowledge, but you want the implementation of this productivity improvement to become your acknowledged job. In other words, this mission you are on, must be viewed as a *management directive.*

Remember, however modest the change you are trying to implement, however desperately it is required in the target area, people will have a tendency to view what you are doing as disruptive. Notice the word tendency, because it is not inevitable that the process will be viewed as disruptive: See the concrete suggestions we offer in Chapters 8 and 10.

Aside from the quality of your own interactions with users, there are some corporate realities that can definitely ease the way. These realities hold just as true in a small company as in one of the Fortune 500 companies. If you have the sanction of upper management, who represent the corporate structure, then it will provide your users with some political incentive to cooperate or at least listen with an open mind. Keep firmly in your own mind the strength and magnitude of resistance you face. Of course, if you do not begin this effort with good tools and techniques, it does not matter if everyone is willing and able to adapt immediately. But you have taken all the steps to ensure that you do have the appropriate tools and techniques; and what remains is politics, people, and the management of the change process.

What lies ahead, then, is a very substantial job that is difficult to achieve. This is why you need the official blessing of management. Indeed, why else would anyone (even your best friends) be willing to take time out of their already busy days? You must arrange for it to be to their advantage (politically expedient) to cooperate to some extent. In fact, the higher in the hierarchy that you and your boss can reach and convince, the more secure your efforts will be. The following story illustrates this point painfully clearly.

Many years ago a friend of mine was part of a team that was developing a new personnel system for a large corporation. This was an interdepartment effort that had received approval by all the directors of the involved organizations. The team had spent 6 months traveling around the country, gathering and analyzing user requirements. Members were in the process of writing the system definition when the president decided to instigate some drastic budget cuts. The new personnel system was one of the most dramatic items on the budget, so he called each of his vice presidents in turn and queried them about the ramifications of canceling the new system. Since the sales pitch (a clear understanding and conviction) had stopped at the director level, not one VP had a firm and convincing answer. The project was canceled (see Figure 4–1).

This story also illustrates the fact that an organization's or indeed even a company's budget is fixed, and therefore people are competing for resources. In order for any level of your management chain to be able or willing to defend to her management or peers the necessity of implementing this particular productivity improvement, she must understand and appreciate it herself. Therefore, every management level that is committed results in a higher probability of obtaining the necessary resources, as well as generally securing the future of the change effort.

This turns our attention away from politics to some concrete reasons to obtain and maintain management support. Such a substantial undertaking cannot be accomplished without some dedicated resources in terms of time and people. For example, you will require a staff to accomplish the objectives you have set for improving productivity. You will also probably need to spend considerable money to purchase the products, associated hardware/software, and arrange the appropriate training. You obviously cannot do this without management approval.

You have already laid all the groundwork for this expenditure and justification for staff in your business case. Thus, this is where we recommend that you begin the conversation when you actually meet to discuss your plans. However, before we cover the topic of the actual meeting, let's take a few minutes to summarize:

1. The main activity in which you will be engaged during this phase is selling.
2. You have this role because successfully overcoming resistance is the secret

to effecting change.

3. Data processing people are unusually resistant to change.

4. You do not have to be unduly worried about these facts, because you are thoroughly prepared by the steps you followed in the previous phases.

5. The first sales pitch will be to upper management.

6. It is critical that you get management commitment at this particular time.

7. You need this commitment at as high a level in the management hierarchy as possible.

8. There are political as well as concrete reasons that necessitate this management support.

9. This corporate sanction will ensure a degree of open-mindedness and cooperation on the part of your users.

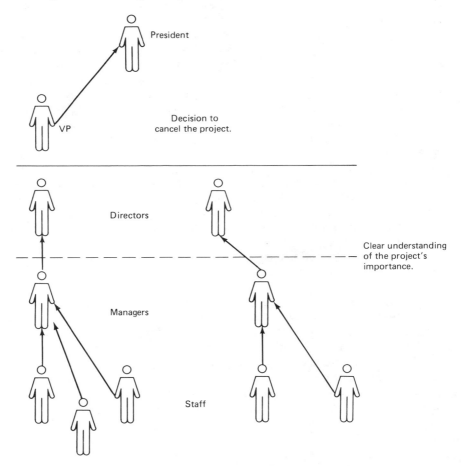

Figure 4–1   Limited communication up the organizational hierarchy.

THE VIEW FROM THE TOP

Unless your upper management is atypical, you can prepare yourself for a trip to an alternate reality. It is a fact that directors and vice presidents view the world of data processing from a different vantage point than project managers and department heads.

Remember when you were traveling around the country visiting work centers so you could estimate the number of processors required for your distributed system? You had gathered a tremendous amount of detailed information, completed a very complicated analysis of the situation, and were finalizing your recommendation. At that very moment you discovered that your director was in the midst of merging the regional areas, and therefore a corresponding work center consolidation was imminent. Naturally your recommendation was now invalid, since it was based on information that was no longer current. The result was that your director's effort required you to rethink your entire study. Did you have a temper tantrum? Of course not! Did you privately curse all people responsible for the bigger picture? Definitely! Reasonably early in your corporate life, therefore, you realized that your current assignment (which surely more than filled your days) was only a small portion of your upper management's life. Moreover, your director's view of the change process will be no different from his view of any other project for which you have ever been responsible. In fact, implementing change may well have a lower priority, since it provides no immediate relief for the myriad crises currently besetting him.

You can employ empathy in this situation just as successfully as you did when you were selecting the products. Remember our discussion in the last chapter in relationship to your users; you can exercise the same skill in relationship to your upper management. Try to imagine how your effort might appear from their point of view. Mentally placing yourself in their position will enable you to determine the best way to approach them as well as to sell them.

ARRANGING THE MEETING

The first thing you must do is arrange a meeting, and this act alone may require considerable persistence and patience. After you have established a date and time with her secretary, be prepared to have the time of the meeting delayed or the meeting deferred to another day. Don't be discouraged, and above all don't take it personally! Keep in mind how busy you are, and how many crises arise in your daily life. Remember that your director has even more commitments, more crises, and many more people to keep track of. For example, her boss (the vice president) may have called her into an emergency meeting to explain why he should not transfer your entire organization from San Francisco to Bismarck, North Dakota. Thus, you should be tolerant of delays, since they can, after all, have a significant effect on your own personal future.

What you do need to do is politely persist: In the case of cancellation, immediately reschedule the meeting; in the case of delay, wait patiently until the meeting can take place. If you have a conflict that will prohibit you from being there after close of work day, we recommend taking strong measures to resolve the conflict and arrange to wait. As a working parent, I know the stress placed upon the family when a schedule that is already strained to the limit is stretched even more. The few times a year that I find myself in this position, I (without hesitation but with guilt) beg my spouse and impose unmercifully upon neighbors to pick up, drive, and keep my kids for a few hours. However distressing this might be, keep in mind that meetings with upper management are not a frequent occurrence, and therefore this type of inconvenience is as rare as it is critical.

If you are persistent and patient and yet still have not succeeded in meeting with the manager, there is one other tactic that we have employed in extreme cases. Next time you see your director heading from her office to the cafeteria, walk along with her and casually mention some arresting piece of news. For example, share the information that a similar productivity improvement at a friend's corporation saved 15%. Another possibility is to point out that when this productivity improvement has been successfully implemented, your organization will be the first in the corporation to have it. The first "commercial" should attract her attention based on budget considerations, while the second is designed to appeal to her competitive instincts. With any luck, you will soon be in the director's office explaining your plans. The point we are making is that a good salesperson must take advantage of unscheduled opportunities as well as rehearsed and organized ones. In your role as a data processing manager, you rarely have all the needed resources, and life in your role as a salesperson will be no different.

PREPARING FOR THE MEETING

Before you begin this much sought after meeting, there are quite a few steps you can take to ensure its success. Obviously you must prepare for this presentation just as you would prepare for any other one. You must create view graphs, flip charts, or slides. My experience suggests that a few quality slides with summary type information will be better received by busy executives than an elaborate and lengthy "dog and pony show"; you should prepare for a brief but formal presentation. You will also need to prepare yourself mentally in several ways. It is almost a certainty that the meeting will be brief, so you will need to make your points quickly. This ability relates to the skill of speaking, which we will cover in detail in the next chapter when we discuss making presentations to your users. However, there is one useful technique we always employ. Before this very important meeting, mentally organize your thoughts into an agenda comprised of the main points you want to make sure you share. Keep this mental checklist in mind during the conversation. Your preparation is not unlike that of an athlete psyching himself for an event: You want to be composed, but very alert.

Another aspect of this conversation for which you want to be as prepared as possible is that upper management is definitely oriented toward the bottom line.

When your people talk to you or in fact when you are communicating with your boss, meeting mutual objectives involves a considerable exchange of detailed information. However, during this meeting, since you do not have much time, you must begin with your conclusions and recommendations. If the director requires or is interested in details, she will stop you and ask questions. In addition, she will probably ask very direct questions and expect decisive answers and even commitments. One technique that you might want to follow involves anticipating her questions. Some of the more common ones that you might expect are these:

1. How many copies of the product do you need?
2. How long will it take you to implement this change?
3. If you get additional resources, can you cut the time in half?
4. How many additional staff members will you require?
5. What particular skills and/or experience will they need?
6. How much will all this cost?
7. How much will it save this year? next year?
8. When can you give me a demo? the other directors? the vice president?

Your experience will be slightly different, but these are fairly standard questions, so give them some serious thought and have answers prepared. Moreover, spend some time framing and answering other questions your own management might initiate.

WHO ATTENDS THE MEETING?

Since it is quite likely that there is at least one level of management between yourself and the director or vice president, it is also quite possible that you may not be invited to the meeting. If this is the case, the situation may not be easy for you to accept. Even if the productivity improvement was an idea of your boss in the first place, surely by now you are the principal change agent. Not only are you the primary zealot, but you are also the person with the knowledge of the organization's needs, of all the products currently available to fulfill those needs, and the details about the product being recommended. You are in reality the best salesperson to secure support, commitment, and resources from upper management. Therefore, it is your job to ensure that whoever does the presenting is thoroughly prepared and armed with as much information as possible. Several scenarios might result in this situation. Since they are quite diverse, we will consider them separately. The first case is the one in which you and your boss are an effective team with a healthy, open relationship. Moreover, it is not his decision to bar you from the meeting, but an edict from the top. Even though you will not be participating in the formal presentation, you might ask if you could be included in the meeting as a technical resource to provide assistance if required. If this is not an option, then all you can do is to work with him so that he can give the best possible presentation under the circumstances.

On the other hand, you may have the misfortune to work for a boss who is insecure enough to have arranged this state of affairs. In that case you will still need to work with him to prepare a quality presentation as well as to ensure that he is adequately informed. There is one additional tactic you can employ under these circumstances, but you must utilize this technique very sparingly and only when the following set of conditions exist. First, you must clearly determine that your boss is not well intentioned and deliberately presenting obstacles. (Be very careful, avoid paranoia, etc.) On some rare occasions, by some serendipity, you may have previously established a rapport with his boss. Then you may consider breaking a sacred code of corporate etiquette and go around your management. The possible adverse affects of this maneuver are obvious and potentially severe, but circumstances (both adverse ones and the serendipity) may make such drastic action necessary and possible.

The other extreme possibility is that when the meeting does take place it happens on the spur of the moment, is quite informal, and has only you and the director in attendance. Have your materials on hand at all times so that you can grab them at a moment's notice. You should probably also bring additional information that you can show if the opportunity presents itself. For example, she may not have read your evaluation report. If you have a copy of the report and time permits, you may be able to share portions with her during the meeting. Although it is highly unlikely your director will be interested in details, such as the product literature, she may want you to walk through the business case and conclusion. Do not forget that facts and figures will be what will sell her or what she will need to sell her peers and management.

THE MEETING

The moment has finally arrived, and you are in middle of the actual meeting. What is certain is that you cannot count on events progressing the way you thought they would. When we were implementing Excelerator, my group and I spent weeks preparing for our presentation to the director. I had been given total flexibility by my boss in connection with the agenda as well as the details of the presentation. The day before the meeting, I approached him, view graphs in hand, and offered to review my materials with him. He politely declined with the comment that he had complete faith in anything I had prepared.

Bright and early the next morning, the meeting took place as scheduled; and all his peers as well as the director were assembled to receive the fruits of my wisdom. My boss began the meeting by writing an agenda on the board that had absolutely no relationship to anything I had prepared. I uttered some small sound of alarm and he glanced my way in a surprised and concerned manner. My panic was undeniable as I rapidly attempted to formulate a strategy to extricate myself from this most unpleasant situation. What I did was to very simply declare that there had been some communication mishap and proceed with the agenda that I had planned. Since my boss and I had an excellent working relationship, there were no hard feelings. Moreover, we did achieve our objectives via the presentation. But I surely did suffer!

To be sure, this story had a happy ending; timing could not have been better, the product was a fine choice for our needs, and the entire management team was progressive. By the end of the meeting we were not only fully funded, but also staffed and commissioned to implement CASE tools in our department. In reality, however, such an ideal conclusion is rare; the most common occurrence is a delayed decision. Typically the director will perceive some benefit, which will be cautiously acknowledged, and you will be informed that the issues of funding and staffing are under consideration. In that case the most practical course of action is to rely on the technique of gentle nudging. Patiently persist by resurfacing your request on an occasional but regular basis, and eventually a decision will be reached.

There is always the possibility that you will have to face refusal, either at the actual meeting or following a period of gentle nudging. If you are confronted with this disagreeable reality, do not be unduly disheartened. Time will pass, managers will come and go, reorganizations will occur, and new products will appear on the market. All you, as a change agent, must do is wait for an opportunity to present itself, and you will soon be able to improve productivity in your organization.

Finally no matter what the outcome, for whatever part you do play, you must exude confidence in order to convey a positive and lasting impression. Answer any questions as directly as possible, with as little hesitation as possible, and with all the conviction you possess. Remember you are not having one of your numerous interactions with your boss, who is probably already more than comfortable with your success rate. If you experience any doubts, relegate them to the back of your mind for when you are alone after the meeting. It is also likely that you and your boss will make the presentation together, and thus you can both answer questions and provide support for each other. But even if this meeting happens on the spur of the moment and you are the only presenter, you do not have to be at all worried: You are well informed, armed with statistics, and absolutely correct in attempting to implement this particular improvement.

SUMMARY

- The main objective of this phase is selling, because the majority of people are quite comfortable with things the way they are and thus do not want to change.
- Not only is overcoming resistance the key to successfully effecting the change process, but it is also difficult to accomplish.
- The first group that you must sell is upper management, and you must have a strong commitment at as high a level as possible.

- Upper management is focused on different issues, so you must use empathy to understand their perspective before and during the meeting.
- Always have the bottom line in mind; management expects and demands direct answers, commitments, and specific recommendations.

Presenting the Product to Your Users

Now that you have obtained the blessing of upper management, there is a potential for a lot of activities to begin all at once. Resist the urge; you must move forward at this phase (as well as any other) in an organized manner. Therefore, we recommend you spend a few weeks (possibly a month) on what we have labeled the *marketing blitz*. However, before we proceed with the detailed steps that are involved, we need to back up a bit and discuss the complexion of your newly formed group. After all, you have just successfully arranged with your management for you and selected others to be dedicated to the productivity improvement you have recommended.

COMPLEXION OF YOUR GROUP

One of the characteristics of this group is that it should be very small; two or three people are optimal, even for the most complex implementation. Actually, this probably is not even a consideration because based on our experience, management will be unlikely to assign more than a few people to such an idealistic effort. They are being asked to invest in something that is not addressing even one of today's problems, but instead is an investment in the long-term future. They will view the whole effort more positively if you do not ask for a dozen staff members. In fact, if you are offered more than a couple of people, politely refuse. I'm sure that this is against all political instinct, but it is essential for success. Think back to the last hot development project you were on (as project manager, project leader, analyst). If it was truly a hot project, the staff was substantial right from the start. Remember the situation during definition and design—people tripping over each other or else dying of boredom. Well, this is similar to that type of environment; there is a great deal of up-front planning required at this time.

Moreover, don't worry about the impression you will make on management when you turn down an offer of staff. We have done this many times over the years, both on development and productivity improvement projects. We have never supported the theory of stockpiling people for the moment when you will need them. When you do require additional staff, you will be able to justify the need and gain the resources. We guarantee that not only will your management understand (now and when you do ask for more), but will even respect you for being motivated by considerations that extend beyond politics.

Given that the group is going to be very small, the members must be experienced. You do not want anyone who has just completed Programmer Basic Training, even the star of the class. You need people who have in-depth expertise in data processing. Set your goal for ten years' experience and settle for nothing less than six. In addition, your staff members must have this expertise in several areas of development. You do not want anyone who has spent a career in one functional area, such as system test or technical support. You want to make sure they will understand the perspectives of all their future users. After all, these users could have diverse assignments from planning to programming. Of course, if the target area is very specific and limited to one function, such as system test, you would try to recruit an individual who is very experienced in system testing. However, this is not the usual case, because most tools and techniques are intended for and can be very useful to many different groups.

It will also be helpful, although it will not be essential, if your staff members have been a part of this particular organization for the last several years. This will facilitate their effective use of the informal network, which is a topic we will cover later in this chapter. Their knowledge and understanding of the organization will also help them when it is time to size up the key players, a subject that will be discussed in Chapter 6. Finally, it is critical that the group have a service orientation. In the last chapter, we mentioned that your users will have a tendency to view you and your group as disruptive. We also mentioned that this is not inevitable, because a lot will depend on your approach (see Chapters 8 and 10). The point we are making here is that there are certain personality types that you should avoid. You do not want people who are arrogant know it alls (even if they do), and you do not want self-absorbed geniuses who are insensitive to the fact that others even exist (let alone have a different perspective). You want people who are thoughtful and analytical (about people as well as user requirements), and who are in general friendly and cooperative. Be careful, though; they must be made of fine mettle, because being an agent of change requires an ability to stand one's ground. It isn't really too difficult to identify the right people; utilize the same techniques you used to select the appropriate person to evaluate the products (see Chapter 3).

Before we begin our discussion of the techniques required to ensure a successful marketing blitz, let's list our suggestions about the complexion of your group:

1. It should be very small in number (no more than two or three).
2. The people should have in-depth (many years) experience in data processing.
3. The people should have had that experience in diverse areas of development.
4. It is helpful if these people also have experience in your particular organization.
5. The group will have a service orientation.
6. This service orientation requires that you select staff members carefully.
7. Personality types to be avoided are arrogant know it alls and self-absorbed geniuses.
8. Personality traits to search for are: thoughtful and analytical, cheerful and cooperative, firm in convictions.

THE MARKETING BLITZ

The major goal of the marketing blitz is to ensure that everyone has some basic level of understanding about the product and its usefulness. Within a week or two, everybody should recognize the name of the product, and you should be flooded with questions. Below is a list of techniques you can use to achieve this heightened awareness:

1. Write a lot of short memos that will be distributed to the whole organization (not just managers).
2. Utilize electronic mail to communicate (briefly) about the product.
3. If possible, show brief videotapes of the product in action.
4. Give formal and ad hoc demonstrations.
5. Give formal and ad hoc presentations.
6. Utilize your informal network.
7. Have group members utilize their informal networks.
8. Have your management (all levels) advertise their support and commitment.

COMMERCIALS

In reality, the first two techniques (written memos and electronic mail) are commercials. They should be brief, arresting, and informative. A typical memo (or mail message) might be as follows:

As you are all aware, considerable attention has been focused lately on a new data modeling technique. Presentations and demonstrations have been given to our director and department heads. Since it is their intention that in the near future we will all be utilizing this technique to improve our systems development, my group would be happy to share information about this product.

We are currently preparing a series of presentations and demonstrations; a schedule with dates, times, and room numbers is attached. If anyone is interested in attending one of these sessions or would like to receive product literature, I can be reached on 981-326-5231.

There are several things you should notice about this memo:

- It is very brief and to the point. Do not risk boredom by rambling on and on.
- It is very specific about how to get information and who to contact. As a user, there is nothing more annoying than to become interested and be unable to obtain details.
- It advertises the commitment of upper management. Do not hesitate to drop names; after all, you worked hard to earn the support.

The other vehicle for commercials, electronic mail, offers several additional possibilities. For example, there is probably some sort of broadcast feature, and it would certainly facilitate spreading the word, if you could add some message that would appear at logon time. In fact, depending on your organization, it might be appropriate to interject some humor. Data processing people seem to thrive on utilizing electronic mail to liven up their daily work life. For example, you might arrange it so that when a group of potential users logon (or boot-up) in the morning, they see the following message:

Attention!!!! Last night we had a couple of maintenance people who are PC hacks and they reformatted your hard disk!!! See Tech Support for information about a file management tool called Norton Utilities (Advanced).

Obviously, this technique must be used sparingly and cautiously. You must gauge the political environment of your organization and be sure that joking does not detract from the product or your effort. However, if your judgment allows for judicious use of humor, it might add a little fun to the arduous and sometimes painful process of change.

The third technique, videotapes, is a method for reaching many people who might be unable to attend a presentation or demonstration. Busy managers might even opt to take the tape home and watch it there. Tapes can also be utilized as part of a presentation, as the introduction or basis for discussion. Since the videotape is an extended commercial, it should also be brief (no more than 15 to 20 minutes), arresting, and informative. If you are very ambitious, you and your group can make your own video. Another alternative worth pursuing is to find out if the vendor has anything suitable for your people.

DEMONSTRATIONS IN THEIR OWN TERMS

The key to success with the next technique, giving formal and ad hoc demonstrations, is to use data that is familiar to your potential users. Moreover, to help you determine exactly what data to use, concentrate on applications that are the cornerstone of your organization. In the case of the new data modeling technique mentioned above in our mythical memo, you might provide demos that use data from the order processing system. The rationale for this choice might include the fact that this system has interfaces to every other system your organization supports (see Figure 5–1).

You will want to limit the extent of data in order to keep the demo simple enough to be brief and comprehensible. Optimally, you could just use a subset of the data that is actually used by the system. However, since you would then be limiting the demo to a specific subset of the order processing system data, the demo might only illustrate a small subset of the product's capabilities. In that case, the solution might be to create a fictitious order processing system. It is not essential that you use live data; what you are attempting to achieve by demonstrating the product with familiar data is to avoid adding extra and unnecessary ingredients. For example, if all the systems your organization develops are for customer management, you do not want to demonstrate a new product using data from a general ledger system. Many people might be distracted by examples that are unrelated to their current assignments and may have difficulty focusing on the product being demonstrated.

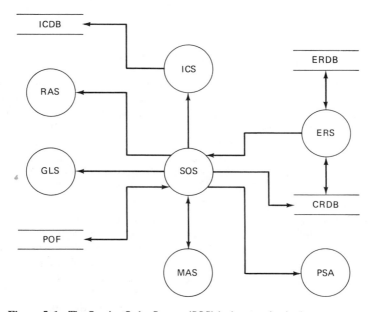

Figure 5–1 The Service Order System (SOS) is the organization's cornerstone.

Whether you use live or fictitious data, a pitfall you must avoid is becoming enamored with the process of preparing the demo. This preparation is fun and it is possible to spend half a career on this, rather than moving on to the difficult jobs that lie ahead. The demo doesn't have to show off every feature of the product or even be particularly elegant. Just keep it simple, brief, and familiar.

PRESENTATIONS—THE COMPLEX SKILL OF SPEAKING

The next technique, giving meaningful presentations that make a lasting impression, depends mainly on properly utilizing the communication skill of speaking. Communication, which is the art and technique of exchanging ideas and attitudes, will become increasingly important in this phase and the next few. Moreover, in order to communicate effectively you must develop the skill of listening as well as speaking. (Listening will be covered in Chapter 6.)

Speaking is a complex skill. There are courses you can take and books you can read on the subject, and if you have the time and budget, it is worthwhile to pursue these options. But since in many cases schedule and resources will prohibit this, here are a few suggestions:

1. Organize your thoughts.
2. Communicate them as directly as possible.
3. Don't digress and ramble.
4. Allow a certain amount of interruption, but ensure you finish making your point.
5. Utilize the method of shifting gears to accommodate your audience.
6. Be sincere; avoid marketing hype and razzle dazzle.

The first three are reasonably self-explanatory; but here is one useful technique we frequently employ. Remember the steps you followed when you were preparing to meet with upper management? You will need to exercise the same discipline prior to any important conversation; that is, mentally organize your thoughts into an agenda. Again as in the case with upper management, keep checking against your main points during the course of the presentation. Focus on your objectives to avoid rambling and digressing. You do, however, want to avoid too much structure and allow for a certain amount of flexibility. With this in mind, let's examine the fourth and fifth items. When you are speaking, whether it is in the context of a formal presentation or an informal conversation, your goal is to ensure that you are understood. One way to determine whether or not you are achieving this objective is to encourage questions. This supplies a mechanism that constantly checks to what extent your audience is with you. A monologue may be easier for you, but you may have lost your audience with the first few words out of your mouth. Since your listeners probably have not developed their listening skills (see Chapter 6), their minds are busily leaping ahead, making assumptions and framing questions. You need to hear those questions as soon as they arise in their minds. If they are way off target, you need to know so that you can present a new slant on the subject, and try again to make your point. Sometimes you even get a pleasant surprise; the questions indicate that not only have you made your first point, but that they are ready for you to move to the next one. In this case, their questions provide a lead-in.

And here is where it is truly important to be flexible. If you have just finished point 1 in your mental agenda and the question leads into point 4, move ahead if it does not hurt anything. You will need to make a mental note to ensure that you cover points 2 and 3. On the other hand, if it would be truly disruptive to skip ahead, you need to indicate that fact. Politely inform the individual that you plan to address that issue in a few minutes, and ask the person to hold onto that thought and raise the questions at that time. Most people don't mind at all and will be totally cooperative. If this is not the case, reevaluate the disruptive aspect of skipping ahead versus having one user who is probably not listening. If you still think it would not be wise to skip the next item, then be polite but firmly insist.

Don't be afraid of interruptions, because you can control both the amount and timing of them, and they can be used to your advantage. Keep in mind that the overwhelming majority of people want to communicate effectively, as do you yourself; those few who are just cantankerous and disruptive you would never have reached in any case.

After you have given several presentations and you are comfortable with the technique of handling interruptions while still achieving your objectives (see Figure 5–2), you will be ready to develop the art of shifting gears. For example, you may have organized your thoughts and mentally prepared yourself to speak to

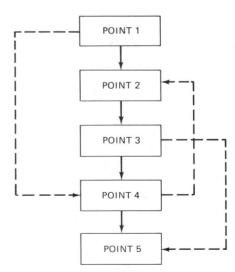

Figure 5–2 Adjusting your mental agenda during a presentation.

a group of project managers. You are about one-third of the way through your presentation, when you realize (by virtue of the questions) that your audience is actually composed predominantly of system testers. If you are cognizant of specific and substantial benefits for the system test phase of development, be sure to mention them. In addition, provide some examples that will illustrate these benefits, and mentally scrap a project management example. You may not be well enough versed or just do not feel confident enough to make such a rapid transition. In that situation, you might consider the possibility of at least stating to your audience that there are definitely ways in which this product can be used to improve system testing. You would also add that you will pursue this with any interested people at a later time. Invite them to leave their names and addresses so they can receive information or the place, time, and date of a follow-up meeting.

SINCERITY AND CREATIVITY—THE MARKETING CORNERSTONES

The final item related to speaking is sincerity, which can be applied to the example we just discussed. Be sure that you do follow through on any offers you make or requests put forth by your users. Provide the information promptly; hold the follow-up meeting as quickly as possible. If the information is limited, provide it anyway. If it turns out that there is no additional information, make sure that you personally let people know. The only way you will ever successfully change the environment is within an atmosphere of trust and confidence. (This will be addressed in great detail in the next few chapters.)

Other aspects of sincerity are also important in the context of presenting the product. You must not engage in marketing hype or razzle dazzle. Never be tempted to promise or even suggest that the product can do something which it cannot. Conversely, you should definitely mention ways to use the product which you have discovered that are not obvious from the literature, but which you are sure will work well for your organization. When we were implementing a CASE tool for analysis, we were naturally focused on the definition and design aspects of system development. One manager in another group discovered a unique application for this tool. His group's assignment was to analyze the manual work flow that accompanied our production systems in the field service centers. He customized the tool's presentation graphics so that certain icons could be used by the people in the field service centers to depict their jobs. Then he further customized the tool so that each icon could explode to a data flow diagram on which the systems analyst could then begin system definition (see Figures 5–3a and 5–3b). This particular application of the tool was publicized far and wide; and its creativity enhanced the appeal of Excelerator in many other organizations. It certainly benefited us in our efforts by virtue of the fact that this unique story did much to heighten awareness of the product.

On the other hand, if there are specific limitations and you are asked about them, state the facts clearly. You probably would not want to go out of your way

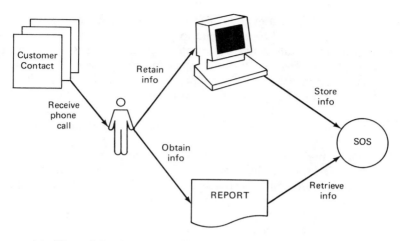

Figure 5–3a Excelerator used for a work center operation flow.

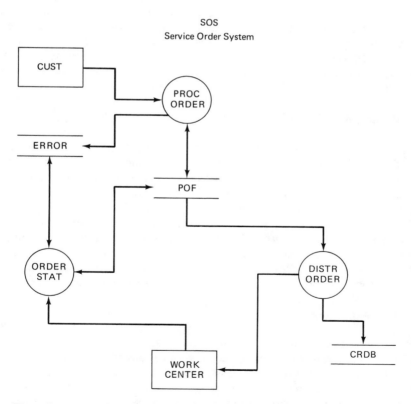

Figure 5–3b Data flow diagram exploded from work center operation flow diagram.

to point them out; you are, after all, a salesperson. Be honest, be sincere, but maintain some political savvy. You also want to avoid razzle dazzle for a legitimate sales reason. If you dwell on any aspect of the product that is merely for show (remember the leaping logo in Chapter 2), then you are no longer employing a soft sell. It is very important that you are not perceived as pushing the product at any time during the entire change process. If you are perceived in this manner, you will lose considerable credibility. Your users will not trust you to have any degree of objectivity, and you will spend your time defending the product and your position.

If you ever find yourself facing these accusations, the best way to proceed is the following. First of all, be honest with yourself—can it be true? If so, step back from the situation and gain some perspective. Remember your original objectives for the target area and dwell on the fact that you had this mission before you ever heard of the particular product you are implementing. In concrete terms, avoid using the product's name over and over as though you were indeed a salesperson. Even though you will spend this time period doing nothing but selling, you never want to be perceived as a salesperson. To help avoid this situation, emphasize the manner in which your people are going to use the product in your own environment. Above all, never argue about any of the accusations; ignore them and proceed with your implementation. You are, after all, too busy to waste time in a way that is as useless as it is senseless. Keep it simple and direct; you have a good product which you thoroughly understand. Just clearly and calmly present its relevance to your own environment.

THE INFORMAL NETWORK

The final piece of advice we can offer about demonstrations and presentations is related to your informal network. Since we have made several references to this network, you may be wondering by now exactly what we mean by this phrase. Any company or department has an official organizational structure that contains a hierarchy of management. There are explicit procedures to follow and specific individuals who have responsibility for authorized duties. However, there is another structure that coexists with the organizational structure based on interpersonal relationships. After all, each individual is not only an employee, but also a person with a rich and complex life that clearly includes many facets outside the duties of a specific job. Friends, relatives, and even acquaintances constitute each person's informal network (see Figure 5–4).

In order to understand clearly the interdependence of the organizational structure and the informal network, let's examine a typical work transaction. Your boss has just agreed to accept your recommendation to set up work stations for your group. He informs you that the paperwork has already been sent to the director for signature to approve the necessary purchases. Now it so happens that you and the director are both members of the school board; therefore, at the next meeting you casually inquire about your paperwork. In the meantime, you have talked

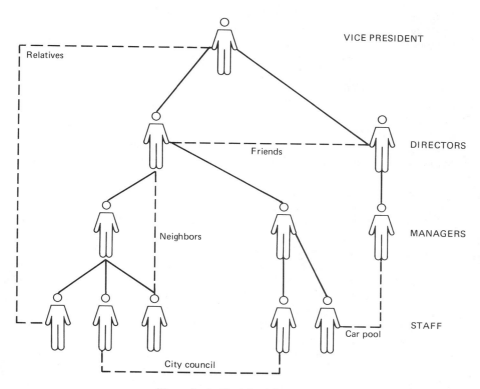

Figure 5–4 The informal network.

to your brother-in-law who works in Purchasing and asked him to be on the look out for the papers and have the associated forms ready to send to the vendors. You have also approached another project manager who is your friend about the possibility of borrowing her technical guru for a week to set up your LAN (Local Area Network). Your friendship is of particular significance because she would not have considered it politically expedient to admit to anyone else that she could spare (however briefly) her most valuable staff member.

What has been accomplished through your informal network is that you have substantially shortened the time required to make your work stations a reality. You will still have to follow all the established procedures and go through all the appropriate channels. Thus the two structures (official organization and informal network) are not in opposition, nor is working through both of them counterproductive. In fact, throughout the entire change process you will have to take both structures into account. You must never cavalierly ignore any formal process; but being aware of and utilizing your relationships wisely will dramatically improve your chances of success.

Let's look more closely at what this means to us as change agents. First of all, you should clearly receive the message that you have considerable influence.

This influence is based upon your network, which is in all probability quite extensive (both within and outside your organization). You must use this influence throughout the entire implementation. In particular, during this phase take advantage of all the relationships you have established. If your buddy stops by to chat about his favorite TV show, don't hesitate to give him a brief demo. In fact, if he walks by your office, call him in and give him the demo. Do not feel that you are conniving or making unethical use of your friendships. Remember, you were careful not only to ensure a good product, but also to gain management sanction. Therefore, supporting your efforts promises concrete improvements as well as being to their political advantage. You are not imposing on anyone; you are just allowing them to be among the first to preview the benefits they will soon be enjoying.

Instruct your staff to do the same thing, because they also have extensive networks. Moreover, they should learn the technique of giving commercials in the form of informal demos. This skill will be useful no matter what their futures bring. It doesn't pay to lose sight of the fact that you are still a supervisor. You must continue to develop your people on this project as you would on any other. Be aware that it may sometimes be hard to keep this in mind, since your staff is so experienced and you will all be so busy. However, you must continue to stimulate their growth; never forget you are a missionary on a crusade and they are disciples, who must be taught many skills and techniques.

Hopefully, your management (all levels) will be spreading information about the product via their own networks. However, you should not count on this in the case of upper management, because as we noted in Chapter 4, they are focused on other issues. But it is reasonable for you to encourage all of them to advertise their support. After all, you worked hard to gain their commitment, and its usefulness can be maximized only if it is an acknowledged fact. You might offer to draft memos for your boss to his peers; or you might ask your director if she would like to include her peers (or possibly her boss) on your distribution list. It is also likely that your boss will want to arrange for you to demonstrate the product to his peers (who, of course, are all already on your distribution list). In fact, some of the upper management groups might also like a brief demo or presentation. It would not hurt to offer this during another casual walk with your director to the cafeteria for coffee.

When you are arranging presentations and demonstrations, you should consider including groups external to your organization. It is a certainty that your network extends beyond your department, and you should capitalize on this fact. Consider this: If you successfully spread the word outside your organization, those people will be likely to tell their upper managers. These directors may very well mention to your director what a wonderful product you are working with and how lucky she is to have such a star on her staff. All this can only strengthen the director's support of your efforts.

Remember, your goal for this phase is to spread the word. The more people (at any level) who show positive interest or offer positive comments of any kind, the better you are able to keep the process of change progressing. The more it becomes an accepted, concrete reality, the more it becomes a fact of life. This will help overcome some of the inevitable resistance. After all, you are affecting the culture of your data processing environment, and although you are dealing with a microcosm, it is nevertheless a revolution.

SUMMARY

- This is the period of the marketing blitz, when you ensure that everyone (not just management) is aware of the product and its usefulness.
- You have staffed your group with a carefully selected small number of experienced people who are thoughtful and analytical, cheerful and cooperative, and firm in their convictions.
- Some of the techniques available to you to heighten the awareness of your users are memorandums, presentations, and demonstrations.
- During this phase you must begin extensive utilization of your informal network, which will serve as a resource throughout the entire implementation.
- The manner in which you pitch your sale will set the stage for the following phases; you must create the proper environment for change.

6

Gathering Information

During the last phase, you were engaged in providing information. The phase of gathering information is a quiet or more thoughtful part of the change process. Your goals during this period are to obtain information from your users, to generally size up the situation, and to set your course of direction.

Let's examine these objectives in more detail. First of all, you must take the time and effort to understand your users' point of view. I know that this statement may seem somewhat redundant. After all, it does seem that all we did during the previous phases was to view reality from their perspective, and this empathy assisted us in literally every step of the way. However, in actuality, we were projecting our own experiences onto our perception of their viewpoint.

EFFECTIVE LISTENING

Remember the project control and tracking tool we mentioned in Chapter 2? At that point we discussed utilizing the art of empathy to determine what will truly benefit your users. We proposed some guidelines for gauging accurately which tools will truly improve their work life. But no matter how much empathizing you do, or how skilled you are at this art, you are still only guessing. To be sure, since you are a project manager yourself, you will be accurate. But you still need to ask other project managers for their opinions. Therefore, what makes this phase different is that you are now going to ask your users directly for their views and listen intently to what they have to say. Moreover, you must never underestimate either the importance or the difficulty of effective listening. Most people would quickly agree that listening is important; however, very few realize exactly how complex an aspect of communication it is.

Listening has been described as a skill that is underdeveloped in most people. We learn to talk and indeed are taught that communication skill, but no one ever teaches us to listen. If you doubt that there is a lack of significance placed on listening, consider the number of books you have seen on the subject versus those written on effective speaking. The bottom line is that currently most of the emphasis in communication is on talking, and there is an almost appalling lack of attention to the skill of listening. Moreover, in the overwhelming majority of books on speaking, there is usually a section on how hard it is to get anyone to listen!

I have taken courses that claim listening is the most important aspect of communication. Too often, when others are speaking we are framing our next sentences or daydreaming about something totally different from the subject at hand. One of the theories I have heard is that the mind processes faster than anyone could ever speak, and therefore your mind leaps ahead. So we need to exercise discipline and improve our ability to listen effectively. To facilitate your development, you should begin by avoiding inadequate listening, as the following example illustrates.

Suppose you are proceeding with the implementation of the project control and tracking tool that has already been mentioned several times. The potential user that you have approached to discuss the tool has launched into a detailed description of the problems the project team is having with each enhancement that is included in the current release of her system. You find yourself mentally drifting away from the conversation and focusing on last night's TV show. Then it occurs to you that you have mapped out a mental schedule for the day that includes talking to six other potential users, and you begin to become very impatient. Furthermore, you used to be the project manager for this particular system, and so you are well aware of all the release problems.

There are several specific ways that you can improve your listening effectiveness in this particular scenario. The first matter for attention is that when the project manager is listing the enhancements and associated problems, you may conclude that she is not addressing your concerns. That conclusion may well be a mistaken assumption. For example, if you listen very carefully to each enhancement and each associated problem, you may see very clearly a possibility for incorporating the tool that will be reasonably easy and will demonstrate immediate and direct benefits. You want to file that information away for use during the implementation. The next item to consider in the scenario is that you must be patient. You cannot hasten this process, and it is much more important to listen to only four users and truly hear what they have to say than it is to reach some quota.

The fact that you had managed the project yourself and therefore could smugly assume that you understood the entire situation illustrates another common pitfall to avoid. You really cannot assume that you know what is being said after a few key phrases and proceed to mentally frame your response. You should also not rely on previous experience to predict what will be discussed. For example, the way the project team develops systems may have changed since you were in charge.

Based on the discussion thus far, it would seem that listening is a passive skill. But that is not totally true. You must also listen to what is *not* being said, and ask questions to draw out the person. This is also critical to the art of being a good systems analyst. Remember how you ensured that you had all the user requirements for the next release? You listened, you persisted, and you asked questions. Asking questions, even vague and half-formed ones, will probably get your user started.

This brings us to the another critical aspect of interactive listening—you must direct the conversation. In order to hear what is important, you must get the user to focus on the real issues. Allow a certain amount of digression. After all, as we pointed out above, she may touch on issues that not only had you not thought of, but that will be valuable later in the change process. However, you must keep bringing her back to what is important until you reach some point of resolution. This requires considerable patience and tenacity, but the technique will become easier the more you use it.

In addition to enabling you to obtain information, there is another important benefit of effective listening. Feeling secure that another person is interested in what we have to say and that we will be heard makes us feel good about ourselves. Furthermore, it motivates us to increase our interactions with that person. If people want to interact with you and your group, that will certainly facilitate the implementation. If you allow your users to express themselves and truly listen to what they are saying, you will provide them with substantial confidence in your sincerity as well as the entire effort in general. Therefore, not only is listening a key to success during this phase, but it will also help lay the foundation for creating the proper environment in which change can take place (see Figure 6–1).

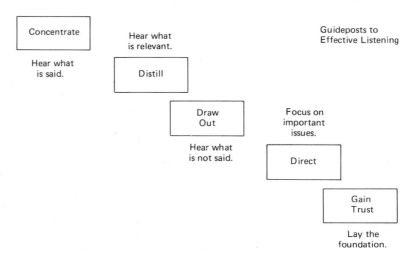

Figure 6–1 Effective listening.

Before we end our discussion about effective listening, let's summarize some of the points we have covered:

1. Listening is a very important part of communicating.
2. Listening is a skill (usually underdeveloped).
3. Applying self-discipline allows you to utilize this skill.
4. Listening is an active as well as a passive skill.
5. The active aspects include stimulating conversation and directing it.
6. Effective listening promotes the proper environment for change.

SUSTAIN WHAT IS ALREADY PRODUCTIVE

Now that we understand the importance and techniques of communicating via listening, let's focus on the concrete types of information you will be seeking. The main thought to keep in mind is that your users are already performing the function you are trying to mechanize and improve. Therefore, they will provide you with valuable information about the following:

1. The aspects of the current method of performing the function that they find extremely useful in achieving their daily objectives
2. The aspects of the current method or operation that they find user friendly, pleasant, and interesting
3. Tasks that they find difficult, repetitive, and time-consuming
4. The fears and concerns they have about the changes you and your group are trying to effect

The first two items are sometimes overlooked—or even worse, the agents of change assume that they know the answers. You want to make sure that you do not omit anything from the current procedures that is inherently productive or especially appreciated by the users. In Chapter 3, we presented an example of introducing a new release planning and scheduling tool. At that time, we focused on ensuring that the tool was compatible with the modality of your organization. That was another way of addressing the same issue: When you select /evaluate a product as well as when you prepare for implementation, you want to retain anything that is positive about the current environment. Therefore, you should make a sincere effort to understand any productive methods and procedures (formal and informal) that are already in place before you plan the future environment.

The third item, which focuses on the unpleasant and thus potentially unproductive aspect of their jobs, should be used to confirm or dispute your original assumptions. Don't worry; it is highly unlikely that you will be way off the mark. You may, however, have to modify slightly which subfunctions you were planning to improve first. The following scenario illustrates this type of modification. Suppose the target area you had selected was definition and design, and you had chosen an analyst support tool to utilize for productivity gains. Your original set of assumptions centered on the functional/processing aspects of development during these early phases. However, after you begin talking to your users, you discover that they are quite satisfied with the current method of defining and designing the functional side of their systems. You also discover that with almost every release there is a major communication mishap that results in incorrect record layouts. What you must do in this case is reconsider which subfunction of the definition and design phases you will begin with. You may then decide to begin the change process (using the same tool) with the data side of development.

ELIMINATING FEAR

The last item on the list is very important for several reasons. The most obvious is that it refers to the whole issue of resistance. One of the most important and fundamental ways you can promote acceptance is to make people feel comfortable about the change and the new way of doing things. In order for you to be able to create this positive environment, you must understand as precisely as possible exactly what it is they fear. This is true because fear really is one of the major causes of resistance. For example, suppose you are introducing a tool to the system test group. Currently, test cases are entered manually by each person in the group. Moreover, each test case is invented by each individual. There is no detailed test script, and group members work from guidelines or a general set of rules. The new tool, which is menu driven, prompts the user with a series of questions, generates the test cases, saves them in files, and then executes them on command. You have projected that considerable savings will be realized with this tool not only because the test cases will be generated, but because they will be reused by many individuals for many releases.

However, when you talk to the people in the test group, you discover that many of them do not view this change as positive and some people are even hostile. After listening (effectively) to what they are saying, you find out they are afraid that many of them will be removed from their present positions. Notice that we did not say they were afraid of losing their jobs. Although you will find a few people who are afraid of this, we do not believe this is a common cause of anxiety among data processing professionals. People are more concerned with losing whatever it is that they value about their current position—the possibility of promotion, no longer working with the peers they like so much, or simply the work itself, which they find enjoyable. If they get transferred or if the group is dissolved, any or all of those concerns could become realities.

You need to be cognizant of and sensitive to these fears throughout the entire process of implementing change. If this is very unlikely to occur, make that unequivocally clear. In the case of the system test tool, there may have been such a backlog that there will not be a reduction of personnel, but rather more (and higher-quality) releases of the system every year. If it is inevitable that the size of the group will be diminished, do not try to deceive the group members.

Although you probably would not want to point this out, it would be a serious mistake to lie if you are asked directly. Remember you still have a long road ahead of you on this particular path and you never want to risk losing credibility. Try to be positive and point out other opportunities that are available both within and outside your organization. Unless your data processing environment is most unusual, there is bound to be plenty of work for competent people. There may be someone you would like to encourage to join your own group when the time is appropriate.

You may find that the only major source of resistance will be the group manager, who is not at all pleased at the thought of managing a much smaller group. This can be a very tough situation, but one option that might be available is to make this person an active part of the change process. For example, make his group the pilot for the implementation, include him in the earliest steps of the planning process, and widely publicize his involvement. You can afford to share the glory; there will be more than enough to go around.

THE INTERVIEW

When they are involved in the activities outlined thus far in this chapter, some people will develop questionnaires and have a formal interview process. Personally I prefer a more informal approach, such as dropping by my users' office (when they are not busy) and engaging them in casual conversation. I believe you will get more information in this type of setting. However, if you feel more comfortable with the questionnaire, either form of interview can produce good results. Whichever approach you choose, consider the following set of sample questions that might serve as a starting point for our project control and tracking tool:

1. For each release of your system, do you currently decompose the phases into activities, and the activities into tasks?
2. If so, do you assign specific people and due dates to each item?
3. Do you compare this to available resources such as machine time?
4. Do you compare this to unavailability of resources such as how much time these people will devote to maintaining the current system?
5. How easy is it to gather, analyze, and maintain this information accurately?
6. Do you then track the rate of progress by running regular reports on a daily, weekly, and monthly basis?
7. How easy is it to run these reports?
8. How useful and accurate are these reports?
9. Who utilizes this information? only yourself? your group? your boss? your upper management? your users?
10. Do you believe this helps you get your system delivered in a more timely manner?

11. Do you believe this improves the quality of your system?

12. What do you find particularly time-consuming and difficult about the process of project control and tracking?

13. What do you find particularly boring and repetitious about the process?

14. What aspects of the current process could you not live without, no matter how marvelous a tool you had?

15. Is there anything about the new tool or your understanding of our plans that concerns you?

For our project control and tracking tool, these questions would be adequate coverage of the four areas we mentioned earlier in the chapter. Of course, in a real situation you would have many more questions, and they would vary from tool to tool as well as from user to user. If at all possible, try to adjust the order as well as actual questions to each individual you interview. As you gain more experience you will be capable of increasing flexibility, which will result in your obtaining more information.

IDENTIFYING KEY PEOPLE

While you are spending this time talking or rather listening to your users, there is another type of information to be assimilated that will be very useful to you during the next several phases. During this period you will have the opportunity to examine the dynamics of each major subset of the organization—to determine where you can anticipate support and where you can expect to meet the greatest resistance. This is the type of information gathering that we had in mind when we proposed one of the objectives for this phase as generally sizing up the situation. Not only will you need to know who will be a supporter and who will be a resister, but you also should determine who is the key person in each group. There is a theory of management, Situational Leadership, that addresses this topic. Every group has a manager, and as you would suspect that is the person with the position power. Every group also has its self-appointed leader who is the individual with the personal power. Of course, it is sometimes the case that the manager has both the position and the personal power, but not as frequently as you might expect.

What is important to you at this time is to determine for as many groups as possible exactly who has the personal power. Then you will mentally select a few of these individuals who appear to be open-minded about what you are trying to achieve. These will be the people you will want to work with during the planning and implementing phases. Moreover, you will mentally note individuals with personal power who appear resistant or even uninterested. Since you want successes early in the change process (more about this later in the chapter), you will want to delay heavy interaction with these people. But be open-minded—it has certainly been our experience that sometimes those who appeared difficult initially became our staunchest allies in effecting change.

BRAINSTORMING

During the time you and your group are interviewing users, you also need to be brainstorming. It is my experience that this is the best and fastest way to reach your third major objective for this phase, setting your course of direction. Moreover, it is important to understand that at this point you are not charged with developing a detailed action plan, but rather a general game plan.

Several years ago, the particular vehicle we chose for improving productivity was instituting mechanized and centrally coordinated data management in our organization. Of course, we had already assessed the need, selected and evaluated the product, and sold our management and users. We were in the midst of listening to the user perspective on the benefits and limitations of our current methods of data administration. Our problem was not that no one was performing data management, but that each group was doing it differently for each phase of the development life cycle. We had data elements that were shared by every system, such as customer id, that had 35 aliases during the logical phases of development (definition, design, etc.) and literally hundreds of aliases in the actual code. This situation was further complicated by the fact that we were dealing with a family of interfacing systems (see Figure 6–2). The obvious result of such an uncontrolled situation was that there were delays in the releases and plenty of dissatisfied users.

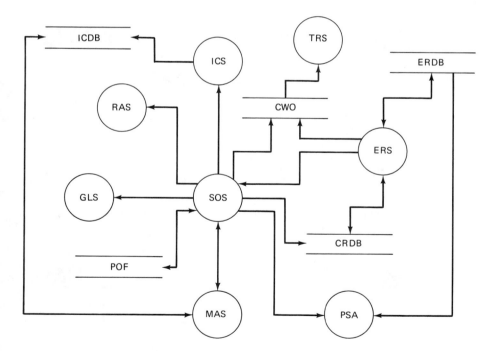

Figure 6–2 Family of interfacing systems.

Two of us were given the opportunity to improve this situation and were finding it fairly easy to interview our users (most of whom we had worked with for years). On the other hand, we were having considerable difficulty figuring out how to begin our implementation. We had discussed the possibility of a top-down approach beginning with a conceptual or ideal view of the data based on our end users' needs. We had also discussed the bottom-up approach beginning with a catalog of the data as it currently existed in our systems. We considered whether it was better to start with production data or have a pilot working in conjunction with a hot new development project. We thought about the pros and cons of beginning with one system we both knew very well versus the pros and cons of beginning with the common or shared data. We created matrices charting user communities and types of data. We filled up white boards in both our offices. We debated and argued every conceivable possibility from every conceivable point of view (see Figure 6–3).

Finally, after about two weeks of this agony, she walked into my office, looked up at the white board on which we had categorized all the information in all of our systems, and had a flash of insight. We began to view everything from a different vantage point and promptly outlined a skeleton. We refined the game plan and went forward to the next phase.

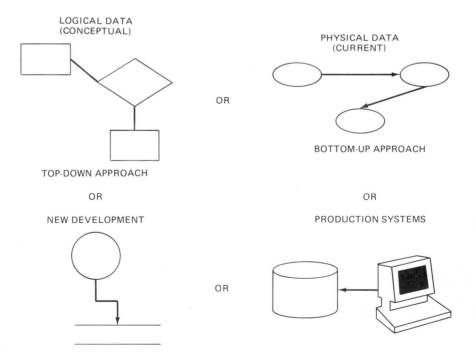

Figure 6–3   Brainstorming the dilemma of determining where and how to begin.

What we decided to do was begin with the interfaces between our systems because they were the most critical, due to the fact they affected two major applications. Moreover, due to their importance, they were the most stable and best documented. Therefore, we began with something very important, and we had a good chance of success. (The idea of moving the implementation in a direction that will result in a series of successes is an important concept that we discuss in detail in the next few chapters.) We also decided to adopt the bottom-up approach. We thought it was important to have an accurate picture of the present reality before designing an ideal view of the world. In that decision we were also largely influenced by the fact that we were part of technical support. Due to our organizational placement we were removed from the end users, which would have made it very difficult to have all the effective interaction necessary to develop a reasonable top-down model. As a matter of fact, we were also removed geographically from the end users, which would have made it even more difficult to produce the ideal model. On the other hand, we were organizationally and geographically close to our programmers, which would be a tremendous asset for the bottom-up modeling effort.

We were quite successful in instituting mechanized and centrally coordinated data management, and whenever we get together we reminisce about the brainstorming. We differ, however, on our predictions for an alternate reality. Looking back across the events that followed, I am convinced that many of the approaches would have worked because the time was right, the tools and techniques we had chosen were good, and we were committed personally and supported by our management. My friend, however, believes that any other approach would have been a false start, and we would have wound up with the approach we took in any case.

The main points to bear in mind about this story can be summarized as follows:

1. This is a difficult, challenging, and exciting step in the process.
2. Because of item 1, it is possible to spend a lot of time on this step. Don't do it; limit the time as you did with other steps.
3. The result was not at all detailed; it probably would not have filled one typed page.
4. Several alternatives will be developed, and more than one of them may work very well.
5. Select an alternative that will be important to management and users alike.
6. Select an alternative with a high probability of success.
7. Consider very carefully your resources and the potential effect they could have (or their lack could have) on any given approach.
8. Make sure you utilize your resource analysis to increase the chances of success.
9. Do not worry about the prospect of selecting an untenable alternative, because it is just a basis for the detailed planning phase and thus can be modified without jeopardizing the implementation.

IMPORTANCE OF THIS PHASE

One of the points you could not have gotten from the story is that this truly is an essential step. If you omit it, you will start the next phase at a serious disadvantage. Exactly why this is so will be explained in the next chapter. But before we move on to planning the implementation, there is a strong advisory that must be shared: There is a high probability that your management will exert pressure on you to shorten or even bypass this phase and the next one. After all, they have been sold, they provided resources (people and time), spent money, and gave their blessing. Now they want concrete results and they want them fast (possibly to keep their management satisfied). Don't even consider this as an option. Reflect on all the valuable information you have as a result of the activities you performed during this phase. Project forward and imagine how much value you will gain from the planning phase. These phases are as essential and critical as any other.

You must explain the necessity of spending this time on pre-implementation activities to your management. If they are unwilling to listen to your explanations of why this is necessary, then you must fight. They would not expect you to begin developing a system by coding it; and they know from experience that when you do circumvent the up-front steps in the development process, it takes more time in the long run. Point out to them that this is similar to taking time to design a system.

They will surely understand this analogy. Promise to recoup the time during the actual implementation, and then do so, even if it means that you work every single weekend and evening. Emphasize that you are in actuality only asking for one more month for this phase and no more than two months for the next one. It is not as though you were adding a year or even six months to the schedule. Above all, have faith and do not back down; they will give you the time. Do not forget that what you are attempting to do (to improve the data processing environment for the whole organization) is important. You were correct in your original assessments, you are an accomplished salesperson, and your management has tremendous confidence in you, or you would not have gotten this far.

SUMMARY

- Your goals during this phase are to obtain information from your users, generally size up the situation, and set your course of direction.
- Information can best be obtained by employing effective listening, which is a very complex and underdeveloped communication skill.
- The types of information you must gather from direct user input include aspects of the current mode of operation that are inherently productive, as well as their concerns about change.
- You must also determine who will be the key players—who is likely to be a supporter or a resister as well as who has the personal power.

- The third activity of this phase is to develop a basic game plan, and the best route to that end is via brainstorming.
- This phase and the planning phase are as essential and critical to the change process as the design phase is to software development.

7

The Interproject Team

One of the most successful methods that we have employed during the planning phase involves utilization of the interproject team. Everyone who has ever worked on a development project is familiar with the project team; we have expanded this concept to include multiple projects to facilitate the change process. Their importance for implementing productivity improvements is fundamentally the same as their importance to any development effort. We will first discuss the relevance of project teams to the development process and then the relevance of interproject teams to the change process.

RELEVANCE OF PROJECT TEAMS

In most data processing organizations, staff members are placed in work groups by function (e.g. system test) as well as application (e.g. payroll system). This grouping of people is necessary from a management perspective; however, it does not usually promote a team approach to development. There is a tendency for individual groups to view the situation as "them versus us," especially when the development of a particular system is not going well. To counterbalance some of the organizational pressures, a project team can be established for the development and maintenance of systems.

The major goal of the team approach is to ensure that all groups consider themselves responsible for all development phases. One group will always have the primary responsibility at any given time, but the others cannot be permitted to be totally uninvolved. For example, the systems analyst has primary responsibility for user requirements, but can also be an active participant in other phases, such as design, test, and deployment. The project team concept requires participation in meetings and other activities throughout the whole development process and therefore discourages the "them versus us" situation which can arise when individual groups view something as "not their responsibility." Everything becomes everyone's responsibility—it is just a question of degree.

The same organizational pressures that sometimes prohibit optimal development of systems can present even greater barriers when you are attempting to change the environment. Turf issues become intensified. It is no longer a question of simply holding on to your empire, because there is a real threat that the entire kingdom may be redistributed into different fiefdoms.

WORKING WITHIN THE ORGANIZATIONAL STRUCTURE

Keeping in mind these organizational pressures, let's examine your role as an agent of change in connection with the organizational structure itself. One of your objectives during most of the process is to work within the structure of your organization. It is not one of your goals to restructure your department, even though during and after the implementation there might be several reorganizations (related and unrelated to the productivity improvements). Obviously the unrelated ones must be survived, and surprisingly enough the related ones must also be survived (see Chapter 12).

Actually, if at the outset you could arrange a realignment to position your department more favorably to receive change, it would not be helpful. You are about to enter into a process during which people will be adjusting to major changes. Therefore, it will be quicker and more effective if the jobs they are performing and the people they are working with (the basic structure of their daily work lives) remain virtually unchanged.

Given the fact that it is in your best interest to work within the current structure, the best methods available to you for achieving your goals are as follows:

- The commitment and support of upper management, which you have already secured
- The utilization of your informal network, which you have already begun
- The formation of the interproject team, which you are about to undertake

This interproject team approach can be very useful during the planning phase of the change process. From every group in your organization that is a candidate for the productivity improvement, there is a potential member of your interproject team. One goal of the interteam approach is to ensure that as many individuals as possible view themselves as active participants in the change process. The more people you enable to have this perception of themselves, the more people you will have who view the success of the productivity improvement as their responsibility.

FORMING THE TEAM

When you are forming the team, the first task you must address is actively seeking commitment of people resources in the form of team members. In general, it is true that you will not have the option of actually selecting all the people. However, based on the management commitment, it is reasonable to expect that you will have significant input. Also, you can and should use all your influence (by virtue of your network) to offer strong suggestions concerning exactly who will be the team members.

There are many issues to consider when you are forming your team, and they will, of course, vary depending on the tool and the target area; but here are some items to address in any case:

- Optimally, the team will consist of representatives from all concerned areas of development.
- It is helpful to obtain representation from as many projects as possible.
- Utilize information gathered, such as who are the key people on each individual project team.
- Accept the option of commitment without representation.

The first item, wide representation, is essential for the development of a viable implementation plan. Although the planning phase would be less stressful if the complexion of your team were homogeneous, the detailed plans, schedules, and standards would not be robust enough to stand the test of time. You must also not limit in any way the breadth and scope of groups that will be represented. We have found that you can never predict who will be the real users of the productivity tool or technique.

In the previous chapter, we described the brainstorming activities associated with an implementation of data management. When we began that particular change effort, we thought our primary user community would be the people who gathered user requirements and provided the system definition. In actuality, during the planning phase the first group to support us was system test, and our very first users of production data were the strategic planners. At the first team meeting, the system test representative eloquently expressed her view of the relevance of data management to the software assurance environment. It was immediately then obvious to us also; any means of accurately portraying any aspect of the application that is being certified is highly beneficial to system test. Exactly why the strategic planners were our first users will be explained fully in Chapter 10. But the point is that since the extent of your user community is not going to be totally clear from the start, do not restrict team membership because of any preconceived ideas.

One group that is often neglected but should definitely be considered as a candidate for representation is your end users. The end user community can be very important, depending on the type of product you are introducing. If you can gain their interest and support at the very early stages of the planning phase, it will facilitate your ability to justify time and expense as you proceed through the change process. We do not mean business case preparation, because that has already been done. However, it is a fact that at many points during the implementation you may be called upon to justify the time and cost already expended, as well as the continuation of such expense. It is certainly our experience that nothing justifies any data processing effort as well as the loud and complimentary voices of the end user community. Moreover, these end users will be the people who will largely drive the priorities of your organization's ongoing and collective development work effort. Therefore, it would certainly be beneficial to the change process if these same people viewed the productivity improvement as one of their priorities.

A prototyping tool is a good example of a product that would be noticeably beneficial to end users. This type of tool offers an opportunity to sit down with users and to have a dialogue that is very specific about what the system will look like. Misunderstandings you might have had will be highlighted, and requirements that were not quite clear to the user may become more refined during the prototyping sessions. For example, you may have thought the mailbox function was supposed to be on the welcome screen; however, when the user sees the prototype, he may decide that this function should be part of the main menu. This discrepancy would have been resolved sooner or later, but it is highly beneficial to have this specification clearly stated so early in the process, and this benefit will also be obvious to your user. Despite beliefs we might have to the contrary, end users are highly motivated to facilitate the on-time delivery of quality systems. Thus, it is reasonable to expect that they may champion your productivity improvement once they are able to appreciate it.

Prototypes (as well as other tools) can also be useful in the sense that the users will have an opportunity for some "hands on" experience with a product. The fact that this product is concrete and was introduced by your group indicates a certain level of competence, and this belief in your competence goes a long way toward building confidence. As we have stated previously, building confidence is one of the prime ingredients in creating a proper environment for change. Thus, there are many reasons to involve your end users early in the change process, if there is any likelihood of their relating to the tool or technique.

Another group you should seriously consider including on the team is operations. For some reason, this group is usually ignored, and yet we have found substantial benefits to be gained by including this group from the beginning. They have a wealth of experience and information to share and a totally different perspective from the other team members. Moreover, in many organizations there tends to be a rift between operations and the other data processing groups; if you are truly committed to building a project team, you will want to bring this group closer to the others. Moreover, unless you are dealing with a PC-based product which you are sure will never require interfaces to computers that reside in a data center, it will be a critical success factor to obtain and maintain the support and commitment of operations.

In Chapter 3 we discussed the importance of centralized groups; in fact, the example provided there dealt with a new editor that improved productivity and as a result dramatically increased on-line usage. The point emphasized in that chapter was the necessity of including technical support in your evaluation. Technical support was involved to provide capacity studies; however, in the same scenario, it was quite obvious that operations would need to be involved in the planning phase so that the increased load on the network could be addressed. With other products it may not be clear whether or not operations needs to be involved, but our experience dictates that it is better to invite them. Then, their representative can accurately determine if there is any impact on the operations environment.

Before we proceed with item 2, project representation, let's take a moment to summarize the suggestions for obtaining wide representation:

- The more diverse groups that are involved, the more robust your detailed plans, schedules, and standards will be.
- Do not have any preconceived ideas about the extent of your user community. Many groups may perceive applications of the product that you did not foresee.
- Consider including end users on your project team. If they begin championing your cause, it will greatly facilitate your effort.
- Consider including operations to avoid the traditional rift between them and other groups.

Item 2, gaining representation from many projects, is also a very important issue to consider when you are forming your team. Since you have worked effectively in the previous phases to obtain substantial management support, it should be relatively easy to achieve this objective. In fact, on some productivity projects, there have been complaints about having too many team members. Our answer to that complaint is that you can never have too many team members! The more people who want to be part of the process, the better your chances of success, because they have already bought into the idea. The buy in indicates that they have accepted the change in some small measure, and you have that much less resistance to overcome.

On the other hand, if a high degree of interest results in a team of 75 people, that is a reality that will have to be managed. All of us have been part of a team and many have been leaders of teams. Therefore, we know that in order to interact in an efficient manner, the team must be reasonably small. So it would seem that we are faced with a paradox: Teams must be small to be effective, yet we cannot limit the size of our team. The solution is to make the official or theoretical team limitless in size, while developing and managing several "working" subcommittees that are the real teams. How to manage this process will be discussed later in the chapter, when we discuss team dynamics and team building.

Item 3 deals with key people as potential team members. If you can clearly identify these key people and they seem even reasonably receptive to what you are trying to achieve, it will certainly promote the success of your effort to have them as team members. Therefore you should utilize all the influence of your informal network to secure a few of these people. Avoid being excessively zealous, however, and consider the possibility that a modest amount of opposition may actually prove beneficial to the project team. For example, if the team has several members with strong opinions that differ somewhat, there is a higher probability that there will be more thought and discussion prior to development of deliverables. The reason is that if two people begin discussing different viewpoints, there is a strong possibility that other team members will also begin to express their opinions. The results will then be a well-negotiated consensus of all their ideas. However, do not carry this advice to the extreme; we are not suggesting that you select only people with strong personalities who are openly hostile to each other. We are merely attempting to suggest that a modest amount of discord is healthy. How to manage this discord will be pursued in the team building section of this chapter.

The final item for consideration in connection with team formation is the concept of commitment without representation, or active versus passive team members. It may happen that certain groups, when approached about team participation, will be too busy or too distracted to participate actively. The manager of the group may be convinced of the efficacy of the productivity improvement, but the current project schedule may just not permit committing a person to participate. There are several issues this situation should suggest for your consideration:

- Accept her decision gracefully.
- Ask if she could personally attend the first meeting to provide public support.
- Ensure that she is kept informed of all team activities, decisions, etc.
- When she approaches you privately with concerns about the decisions, listen effectively.
- If appropriate, act on her suggestions, even if it is inconvenient.

The main thing to consider is whether or not you really have support. If so, then you need to nurture it just as surely as you would if the person was actively participating. You must also react to her concerns, because if the decisions made by the team have serious flaws, it is better to face that fact and deal with it during the planning period than later in the implementation. On the other hand, if you do not have support, then pressuring her to send representation will accomplish nothing. In either case, you must accede to her wishes. Finally, you must consider all the possibilities available to you in terms of who is on the team as well as the specific form that their participation may take (see Figure 7–1).

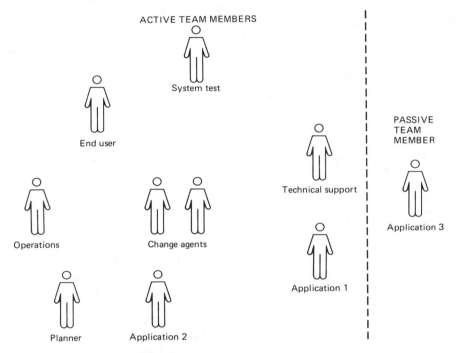

Figure 7–1 The issue of who is on the team.

TEAM MEETINGS

Now that you have successfully formed a team composed of both active and passive members, the next thing you need to do is clearly communicate to all interested individuals in your organization the following facts:

- You have formed a project team.
- The purpose of the team is to develop an implementation plan for the entire change process.
- The time and place of the first project team meeting.

You should hold project team meetings on a regular basis. We recommend once a week initially, for the following reasons. The team has considerable work ahead of it, so the team members must meet fairly frequently. However, it would be difficult for them to meet more often than once a week because your group will need some time between meetings to document and synthesize information provided by all team members.

These project team meetings can be a powerful means for coordinating the planning and implementation of the productivity improvement. They offer an arena for gathering and understanding information that affects the implementation's progress, such as a new user requirement that was not discovered during the information-gathering phase. The team meeting is the proper context for uncovering critical activities that are not getting accomplished, discovering the reasons, and then arranging for labor and support to reverse the situation.

On the other hand, these meetings can be frustrating and dissatisfying experiences, and in extreme cases even a complete waste of time. The difference will depend upon you. To ensure that your meetings are useful, you should adhere to these guidelines:

1. Keep your meeting reasonable in terms of time—a half day maximum.
2. Have a specific agenda and follow it as closely as possible.
3. Publish the time and place of the meeting and the agenda well ahead of time.
4. Publish any items of interest as soon as possible after the meeting.

Items of interest might be schedules or activities that the team agreed upon and the names of the persons or groups designated as responsible. Publishing information (both before and after meetings) is important for several reasons. As we noted in the case of the over-worked manager, not all team members may be able or willing to attend all meetings; however, they need to be informed not only of what has taken place, but also of what will be discussed at the next meeting. Then, if there are particular issues about which they are concerned, they can attend a specific meeting and share their opinions. If the meeting has already occurred, they can still share their concerns with you. Of course, you will always welcome their input and if necessary reopen that specific issue at the next project team meeting. Again, as we stated above, you need to address potential and real problems as early in the change process as possible.

We also have some advice to help you keep your meetings reasonably short while still adhering to the original agenda. There will be a natural tendency on the part of team members to digress, and a certain amount of this is healthy in terms of team building. People will begin to feel comfortable expressing themselves, and they will become confident that the others are listening. Problems will have a chance to surface that might not have been uncovered until they caused tremendous repercussions in the change process. But you must bring people back to the main issues and reach some point of resolution for each item on your agenda. One technique for achieving this is to establish action items for issues that cannot be resolved easily at the meeting. Another technique that can be utilized when a team member becomes concerned with an issue that does not affect the others is to offer (and politely insist if necessary) the option of a private meeting following the team meeting. Always remember that you are running the meeting—be polite and flexible, but firm.

BUILDING THE TEAM BOND

It is also important to remember that you must truly work at building a team during, before, and after the meetings. To begin with, you should arrange to have a conversation with each potential member prior to the first meeting. This provides you with an opportunity to explain your objectives and to answer any questions the individual might have.

During the meetings, you will be strengthening the team by the manner in which you conduct the meeting. Here are some of the techniques already identified, along with some new ones:

1. Clearly define the objectives of the team and their importance to the organization.
2. Eloquently communicate the commitment of all levels of management to this change process.
3. Provide a structure for the meeting, in the form of a well-thought-out agenda.
4. Be flexible with the agenda so that the ideas and concerns of the team can surface.
5. Ensure that every team member has an opportunity to express himself.
6. Listen effectively to every team member throughout the entire meeting.
7. Utilize the ideas, experience, and knowledge that are being expressed.
8. Never allow any team member to be intimidated by other team members.
9. Understand the interpersonal dynamics between individual team members.
10. Capitalize on the positive relationships and diffuse the negative ones.

Another thing that you must do is maintain the team bond from meeting to meeting. One method that helps achieve this objective is to make sure you have some interaction with each member between meetings. This interaction can take the form of stopping by the person's office to share an idea that you will present at the next meeting or to hear his ideas about how the planning phase is proceeding. This one-on-one meeting does not have to be long, but you need to give the other team member your full attention and not just rush in and rush out. If your offices are not all in the same building, a phone call is fine. The main point is that you need to believe you are all truly united in a common effort, and then share this belief, both during and between meetings.

The next technique for maintaining the team bond between meetings has the potential of realizing additional benefits for the entire productivity improvement. You should assess the experience, abilities, and interests of all the team members. Then, when action items or scheduled activities are assigned, try to arrange for people with complementary assets to work together between meetings. For example, there might be a hardware expert from operations and a software expert from technical support who are friends and on your project team. There might also be an open action item that deals with projections for capacity in the time frame immediately following the implementation of your product. This item would be a good candidate to assign to both the technical support and the operations representatives. You might include the team member from the database administration group who has privately expressed a desire to you (during a one-on-one meeting) to learn more about the hardware your product will use. The result of this assignment might be beneficial in many areas:

1. It is highly likely that the cooperative effort of the three people will produce very good capacity projections.
2. They will probably provide some informal cross training for each other.
3. This will be a bonding experience, and the whole team effort will be strengthened.

Needless to say, you will want to avoid grouping people who dislike each other or who have overlapping skills and experience. However, occasionally the needs of the project may force such groupings. In that case, you can ease some potential tension or lack of experience by remaining closely involved with this subgroup.

As we mentioned at the beginning of this chapter, the whole concept of subgroups is one that lends itself to accommodating extremely large project teams. The idea is to assign responsibility for each scheduled activity, action item, and deliverable to a subcommittee. You and your group will manage and track the progress of each item, and if necessary become involved with different groups whenever they are having difficulty. The project team meetings then become an arena for providing schedule status and review of critical deliverables, and therefore would probably not need to be held more than once or twice a month. The subcommittees are where you will provide team building and team support (see Figure 7–2).

Another piece of advice on the subject of team building is that it is very important to feed the team. Provide coffee and rolls in the morning, soda and cookies in the afternoon, and always have lunch brought in. Going back to ancient times, man has understood the importance of breaking bread together; capitalize on this

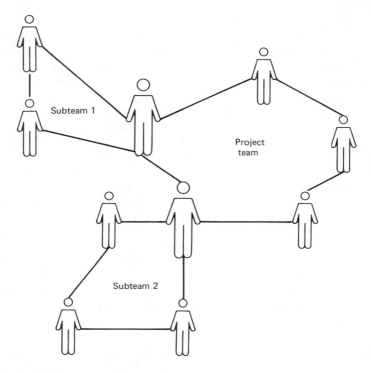

Figure 7-2 Team management is balancing size and efficiency as well as forging the team bond.

fact. Catering lunch is a key factor to promote team bonding; it guarantees that there will be at least one hour of fellowship for the entire team every single week.

TEAM LEADERSHIP

One point that needs to be clear in your mind concerns team leadership. Every team needs a leader. Since you have formed the team and are the person who is keeping the team together and on the right track, you have that role. In Chapter 6, we mentioned the concept of position power and personal power in the context of situational leadership. Both types of power apply to your leadership role in the team. Since you have been given the mission of implementing this productivity improvement at a fairly high management level, you certainly can command a certain amount of position power. However, the people on your team are the members of some other manager's group, and thus they are an essential and critical resource that is not directly under your control. In fact, there is considerable potential for them to be dealing with a set of conflicting priorities. There are several ways in which you can avert the apparent hazards. First of all, you should utilize all your personal power within the team arena. You must convert these people to your crusade for improving the environment; they must believe in the mission; and they must perceive you as their leader in activities that will accomplish this collective objective. Do not falter in the face of such a task; remember your own commitment and your sales abilities. Once they are committed to the cause, they will influence their managers to maintain and even increase their team involvement.

The other method at your disposal to obtain and maintain this critical resource is to utilize your influence with their managers. Do not forget that many of them will be part of your informal network, and therefore you can press a little if these other managers begin to pull team members away during their own group crises. In addition, you can and should utilize your influence with other managers who are not part of your network. Do not hesitate to point out the advantages of the productivity improvement for them personally, in addition to the potential glory for them for being associated with it, and by all means reiterate the support of upper management.

Let's summarize the techniques available for building and maintaining the team bond:

- Maintain regular one-on-one contact with all team members between meetings.
- Share your objectives, commitment, and enthusiasm during and between meetings.
- Conduct the meetings in such a way that every team member feels comfortable about expressing himself.
- Truly utilize the ideas and knowledge of the team members, and never commit the sin of politely listening and then following your own preconceived notions.
- Be aware of and act upon both the positive and negative dynamics between team members, in terms of grouping people to work together on action items.
- Feed the team to promote pleasant and regular fellowship.
- Never forget you are the leader of the team. Utilize your position power, personal power, informal network, and management commitment to keep the team intact and on target.

DURATION OF THE TEAM

The final comments about the project team have to do with its duration. This interproject team is unlike the development project team in a fundamental way. The development project team has a reason for being for as long as there is a system that is growing (new development or major enhancements). The team leader (who is usually the project manager) has as an objective keeping the team as intact as possible. She does not want to lose their collective experience, nor does she want to lose the team bond; a lot of effort was invested to develop both the expertise and the team spirit.

On the other hand, the interproject team cannot and should not be an ongoing team; it has a very specific purpose with a very definite time frame. When the objectives have been achieved and the time is right, the team must be dispersed. (Exactly when this time occurs will become clear as we proceed.) Moreover, this time will occur long before the change process is completed, so it is conceivable that you will, somewhere along the way, require another interproject team. In this case, you may be wondering why you should not just maintain the original team. This is not a viable option. You are a proponent of improving productivity, of making your environment better, and thus it would be contradictory if you wasted resources (people and time) along the way.

SUMMARY

- The interproject team is necessary to counterbalance organizational pressures and to effect the change process within the existing organizational structure.
- You must encourage representation from many different types of groups (system test, planners), as well as from many different projects.
- Diverse and widespread representation will produce a robust implementation plan and increase the number of people actively participating in the change process.
- The team bond, which will be established by you as the leader, must be maintained during and between meetings.
- Unlike the development project team, the interproject team brought together for the change effort cannot be an ongoing team; you will have to disband it in the spirit of productivity.

8

Planning the Implementation

When you are planning the implementation of a productivity improvement, you must perform the same tasks as you would if you were planning for the development of a system. You must have a strategic plan and a tactical plan, as well as a detailed set of plans for the actual implementation. The reason that you must keep the long-range perspective in mind is directly related to both the potential future ramifications of effecting change and the time that will be required to complete the change process.

THE STRATEGIC PLAN

There is no doubt about it: If you are successful (and you will be), not only will you irrevocably change your present environment, but you will also have tremendous impact on the future. Thus, you must consider what the future scenario would be without any planned productivity improvement, as well as what it will be with the changes you have envisioned. The first thing you must do is take stock of where your organization (and indeed your entire company) is headed. To achieve this objective, you might consider utilizing your informal network, which may well already extend into the corporate planning groups. (If you do not have connections with these centralized groups, establishing them should become a priority, because it will be very important later on in the change process.) You do not need an exhaustive study of the strategic direction of your company, but rather high-level information so that you will have some general sense of the future for positioning purposes. It will also facilitate your ability to position the implementation plans for the future if you are aware of any near-term and long-range major organizational changes that are being considered. This task is quite vague, and really all you can do is keep yourself linked into the rumor mill and remain as politically attuned as possible. We do not recommend wasting time or energy on this, however; we are suggesting that if you do come across this type of information, factor it into your planning equation.

The final and most important area that you must take into account for strategic planning is the direction in which technology is headed. We understand that this is about as easy as building a crystal ball and then trying to become psychic. However, there are some methods that are readily available to all of us. The most straightforward and obvious option is to keep yourself informed of the current technological situation. Of course, that can become a full-time job. Let me share one way I deal with the dilemma. I do make an effort to read one article a day from a trade journal, and I try to avoid always referring to the same one. More important, I rely heavily on friends and associates for information.

All of us know people who spend hours each day gathering information about the current state of technology and where it is headed. These are almost always the same individuals who spend considerable energy analyzing and predicting future technological directions. By all means utilize this excellent resource; there is no need to perform tasks personally that are already being performed by others. Moreover, this technique is merely an extension of skills that you employ every day as a competent supervisor; you delegate a task to an employee and then have that person brief you on the results. The difference here lies in the fact that there is no need to delegate or request a briefing, because your "techy" friends are already performing the task. Moreover, they actively seek opportunities to and thoroughly enjoy doing the briefing.

Let's pause and summarize areas to consider for strategic positioning of the change process during the planning phase:

- Attempt to assess reasonably accurately the strategic direction of your organization and company.
- Be as aware as possible of any major organizational changes that might affect the productivity improvement you are implementing.
- Keep informed of technological directions that might affect your efforts.

THE TACTICAL PLAN

Now let us examine the length of the change process and its relationship to tactical planning. Do not delude yourself about the amount of time that will be needed to complete the change process. The effort required to bring about the cultural adjustment that results from the successful erosion of resistance will take years. On the other hand, do not view this fact with discouragement, because you will realize substantial benefits within a matter of months. Moreover, many methods for achieving these multiple intermediate results will be outlined in several chapters (including this one). The fact is that although you must give some thought to developing detailed implementation plans for the next 6 months, you must also give some thought to where you want to be in a year or two. Then you can formulate some high-level but specific items that comprise your objectives from a tactical perspective.

All this strategic and tactical planning should be done solely by you and your group; there is absolutely nothing to be gained by involving the interproject team in this effort. Indeed, you do not want to spend a great deal of time and energy on these steps. They are important as points of reference to be used during the detailed planning activities. Some items to bear in mind about tactical planning are these:

- Since the entire change process takes years to complete, you need to consider where you want to be in one to two years.
- You do not need to develop a detailed tactical plan; a simple list of your objectives will suffice.
- Do not involve the interproject team, because you do not want to spend substantial resources on this.
- Even though the time and effort to prepare the tactical plan should be minimal, it is important and should not be omitted.

STRATEGIC AND TACTICAL PLANNING—AN EXAMPLE

To provide some concrete examples of what all this means in practice, let's look at some of the strategic and tactical planning we used during our implementation of data management. Initially we were given the charter to provide data management tools and techniques for only one-third of our organization; however, we perceived from the very beginning that the function we would be performing would naturally extend to a part of the department that was outside our scope. Therefore, we included on our interproject team representatives from these other groups. We utilized information provided by these people as well as our own understanding of their part of the organization to ensure that everything we planned would also accommodate their needs. We were correct in our assessment, and after the initial implementation we did become responsible for the whole department. Moreover, we were able to incorporate these areas without massive disruption to previously developed methods, procedures, standards, etc.

We also sought and maintained close contact with the group that was setting corporate data policy and standards. We obtained information about their activities and shared our plans to safeguard against major and unpleasant surprises in the future. During our implementation, we heard a rumor that there was going to be a major corporate restructure that would result in our organization's merging into another line of business. We were well aware that the data management groups in that line of business used totally different tools and techniques. Utilizing our informal network, we established an information exchange day. By the end of the day, all sides were able to conclude that although different tools were being employed, all techniques were fundamentally consistent.

Figure 8–1 contains a graphic summary of the process of involving many people for strategic and tactical purposes. It is worth noting that all the activities described here required very little time and people resources, yet the return from the minimal effort was substantial. We did not spend hours or days poring through documents or chasing vague rumors, but we did pay attention to peripheral activities and prudently utilized information to avoid considerable restructuring of the implementation further on in the process.

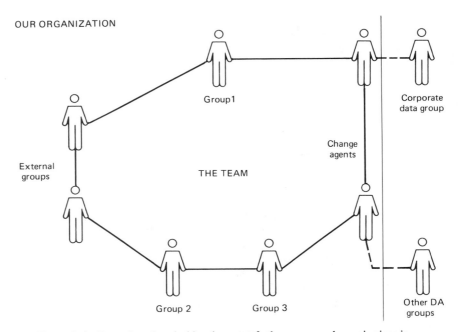

Figure 8–1   Strategic and tactical involvement of other groups and organizations in team interactions.

DETAILED PLANS—HOW TO DEVELOP THEM

Having addressed the strategic and tactical planning process, we can now turn our attention to the main work of the planning phase. The major activities of this phase involve the development of the detailed implementation plan, which will be performed within the arena of the newly formed interproject team. Moreover, although this is a pre-implementation phase, there are concrete deliverables. But before we describe these deliverables in detail, we need to address the manner in which they will be developed.

In the gathering information phase, we stated that you needed to "set your course of direction" prior to beginning the planning phase. This basis for the planning phase is a prerequisite because of team leadership issues. You can not expect to lead the project team effectively or have the team members view you as having the personal power unless you begin with a clear idea of where you are headed, and have a basic route to get there already mapped out. Furthermore, it is imperative that you and your group prepare a draft version of each deliverable prior to the project team meeting that will address that particular deliverable. The draft does not have to be elaborate or even complete, because it is intended as a basis for discussion only. However, it is truly essential to have something concrete to begin each meeting with, or you run the risk of the meeting becoming a group grope. You can begin with your group's proposal, and then you will need to draw from the collective expertise of the team. The result may be a deliverable that does not even remotely resemble the draft, and that is perfectly acceptable.

Do not worry about having a polished and finished document to present; a rough draft is quite appropriate. Actually, you should concern yourself more with the possibility that the proposal will be too polished and will inhibit the other team members from freely contributing to the final product. You must also guard against the possibility that your group will have extended their efforts so far that they will not be open to team suggestions. However, you are the team leader, and you will ensure that your group is prepared with a draft and that the team truly develops it into a final product.

The manner in which the planning will be performed can be summarized as follows:

- The basic game plan was established in the gathering information phase to enable you to begin your team leader role effectively.
- To avoid group gropes you must begin the preparation of every deliverable with a draft document.
- Unless emphasis is put on the draft aspects of the document, the team may not freely contribute and thus produce a quality final product.

POLITICAL HAZARDS

Before we proceed to the deliverables themselves, we must make you aware of some political hazards that have a high probability of surfacing at this particular juncture. Up to this point, no one would have conceived of trying to gain control of the change process. Prior to this phase, all your efforts were directed toward educating people at all levels as to the importance of your activities. Now, however, you have successfully convinced many people that the change is critical in a very real sense for the future well-being of your organization. The natural result of such awareness is not only that people will view it as politically expedient to follow the leadership you are offering, but also that some individuals will perceive that it would be even more expedient to lead the effort themselves.

This type of power politics may emerge any time in the change process, but often the first arena is the interproject team and the first battle is during the planning phase. There are also many ways that people will make an effort to usurp your power; the most direct one is attempting to gain enough personal power to seize control of the project team. Actually this is not a situation that you need to fear because you have the position power granted to you by upper management, and that is sacrosanct no matter how much personal power another individual gains. On the other hand, you do want to retain as much of the personal power as you can, because it will not benefit the team bond if meetings consist of a series of power plays.

There are some coping mechanisms that frequently alleviate this type of situation. For instance, sometimes it helps if you can concede a few minor points. This deferring to the other person may reduce their perception that it is a "win lose" situation. If their ideas (or any team member's ideas) can be utilized, by all means cooperate. Avoid unnecessary confrontations; there will be enough issues over which you will have to do battle. Remember that your objective is to produce the deliverables and plan the implementation, not impose every one of your own ideas on the change process. We will provide some very specific examples of when to cooperate and when to confront when we describe the establishment of standards in the next chapter.

Another type of power struggle you will sometimes encounter is of a more passive nature. Some individuals will not confront or even argue with you or any other team member, but will instead persist in following their own direction even though it is in direct opposition to everything the team is developing. This kind of behavior is wasteful and counterproductive; and when the team becomes aware of it, quite demoralizing. In general, the techniques described above will not improve this situation, and our recommended course of action is to remove the person from the team. If removal is not an option, then you must just outlast the problem. Remember the change effort will move forward, and eventually you will have more ability to enforce the standards, procedures, or whatever it is that is not being followed. We will refer again to this specific situation in Chapter 12, when you will be in a position to resolve this conflict.

In every one of these political struggles, what you must really remember is that you do have the authority to proceed with your mission, and you are the team leader. But, as the change process proceeds, you will face problems that you will not be able to readily solve. You and your group will have to accept and live with some frustration and ongoing concerns. All that is really possible in unresolved situations is to exercise authority and leadership wisely. Keep trying to reach the difficult team members, persist gently in including them, solicit their suggestions, and accede to their best recommendations. At the same time, you must protect the rest of the team from rugged individualism for its own sake or the political maneuvers of attempted takeovers. If you do not maintain control of the situation, you will find yourself and the team on the road to anarchy.

Be patient, kind and firm, and you may find that eventually your good intentions will become apparent and the difficult person will be converted. If not, at least you will have diffused the situation as much as possible and spared the team anxiety. You must constantly endeavor to maximize the progress and quality of the change process. But you must also strive to minimize friction and disruption for the sake of all the people who will be heavily involved or even touched by the process.

The final political battlefield of which you should be aware is that with the increased popularity of your effort, your management at any level may also be struggling to retain control. The only participation that you can have in that political arena is to keep your management chain well informed so that they will have the ammunition to fight their battles. If they lose their war, you may be reporting to another boss, but chances are excellent that your group will be moved as a unit and the change process will continue.

Reorganizations can indeed jeopardize many aspects of your implementation, as we will describe in Chapter 12. At the very least they will slow down the change process. Therefore, anything you can contribute to help avert them will be beneficial to everyone concerned. It is important to note, however, that in a certain sense you cannot really personally lose any of these political battles. It was your conviction that began the implementation, enabled a successful sale of the product, and brought the productivity improvement to this stage. Your enthusiasm is undoubtedly a critical success factor; you are firmly entrenched in the change process; and it would not be easy for you to be replaced. However, you still must maintain as an objective avoiding conflict and neutralizing the political overtones, because they can seriously drain the efforts and progress of your group, your team, and yourself.

Let's pause a minute and summarize the political battles you might anticipate during this phase:

- Due to the increased popularity of the productivity improvement, team members may try to take over your role as team leader.
- The takeover effort may be in the form of an individual using personal power to usurp your position.
- You may also encounter passive resistance in the form of extreme nonconformity.
- You have position power (due to management sanction) and personal power (steadily increasing), which secures your authority.
- You want to assist your management, if they are facing similar battles, because reorganizations will slow down the change process.
- In general, you need to minimize all disruptions, or the change process will be seriously impeded.

DELIVERABLES

Having spent considerable time on the mode of producing deliverables and the politics involved, we will focus our attention on the deliverables themselves. Here is a list of the most common outputs of the planning phase:

1. Gantt charts that reflect work breakdown structures (phase, activity, and task) to allow for time and resource scheduling, availability, and work status reports
2. Dependency diagrams to highlight the critical paths
3. Standards, naming conventions, and methodologies to be followed by users
4. Documented draft description for roles and responsibilities of both users and change agents
5. Documented draft procedures for managing the emerging environment, e.g. change control and version control

The first item, the Gantt chart, is the facility that allows you to accomplish the following:

- Division of the effort into its phases
- Specification of activities within phases that must be performed
- Subdivision of these activities into tasks
- Identification of who is assigned to each task
- Identification of time (number of days as well as elapsed calendar time)
- Tracking the status of each phase, activity, and task

Several PC-based tools are available to automate these planning activities. The report from our data management experience that is provided as an example (see Figures 8–2a and 8–2b) was prepared by PW (Project Workbench), a tool we often use for planning. Figure 8–2a illustrates an activity (Load SOS ERS data) and its associated tasks (e.g., Collect Documentation, Analyze Information, and Input Records) for the implementation phase (IMPLEMENT) of our data management effort. The advantage of utilizing a tool is that you can easily change the inputs, and then the resource scheduling (Figure 8–2b) is dynamically performed. In addition, the numbers associated with the Gantt chart are calculated for you, stored, and are available for reporting at various levels of detail. All this information will be very important during the entire implementation for determining exactly what is on or behind schedule. Figure 8–2a also provides an example of status information; notice that some tasks are depicted on the timeline with double lines (denoting a completed status), while uncompleted tasks are depicted with a single line.

      Lines that begin with a C indicate that the task is part of the critical path. This capability of PW is valuable because you can visually depict the minimum amount of time required to complete the project, no matter how many additional

PROJECT: Data Management

Data Management	Da	Who	January 1988				February 1988				March 1988				April 1988	
			4	11	18	25	1	8	15	22	29	7	14	21	28	4	11	18
IMPLEMENT																
Load SOS ERS Data																
Collect Documentation	5	SM														
Analyze Information	10	BB														
Input Records	5	AS														
Review Rec for Accuracy	10	SM BB														
Correct Records	5	AS														
Input Elements	10	AS														
Review Ele for Accuracy	10	SM BB														
Correct Elements	7	AS														
Distribute to Users	3	BB														
Analyze User Input	13	SM BB														
Input Corrections	8	AS														

Figure 8–2A. This diagram is a sample gantt chart from our data management effort.

PROJECT: Data Management

Data Management	Da	Who	January 1988				February 1988					March 1988				April 1988		
			4	11	18	25	1	8	15	22	29	7	14	21	28	4	11	18
RESOURCE SUMMARY																		
UNASSIGNED	0.0	X	5.0			2.0	3.0		3.0	2.0	3.0		4.0	4.0				
SALLY	5.0	SM	2.0	5.0		2.0	3.0		3.0	2.0	2.0		2.5	2.5				
BARBARA	5.0	BB			3.0	3.0	5.0	5.0	5.0	5.0		3.0		4.0				
ALAN	5.0	AS			2.0							2.0			4.0			
TOTAL DAYS			7.0	5.0	5.0	7.0	11.0	5.0	11.0	9.0	5.0	5.0	6.5	10.5	4.0			

FIGURE 8–2B. This resource summary, companion to the gantt chart, indicates availability (5.0 days per week) and days already allocated for specific weeks.

resources upper management tries to force on you. Figure 8–3a is a dependency diagram and Figure 8–3b is a CPM network.

In the data management case, it is clear that you cannot begin to Input Elements until you have completed Correct Records. These diagrams also indicate the number of days past the due date that can be tolerated for a particular task without affecting the end date. Thus it is apparent that there is a built-in slippage period of five days for each task. See the last number in the boxes representing these tasks on the CPM network (Figure 8–3b).

It is worthwhile to employ productivity tools and techniques wherever possible throughout the change process. Of course, the primary reason is because it will improve implementation in terms of both speed and quality. In addition, it does add substantial credibility from your users' perspective that you are sincere in your efforts to improve the data processing mode of operation. The most noticeable and beneficial employment of productivity tools and techniques is when you are able to use the product itself during the implementation. For example, you might use PW to plan its own implementation in your organization.

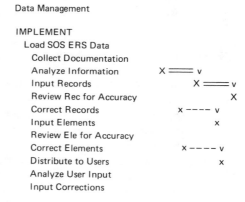

Figure 8–3a Note that on this dependency diagram (companion to the Gantt chart), the critical path is highlighted by double lines.

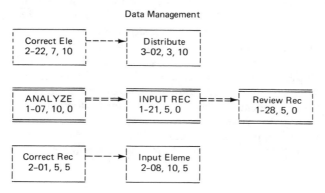

Figure 8–3b The CPM Network indicates critical path (middle set of boxes), start dates, duration, and slippage.

Discussion of the third item, standards, naming conventions, and methodologies, will be bypassed for the time being. We believe their judicious use is a critical success factor for the implementation of any productivity improvement, and thus we devote an entire chapter to the subject.

The next item on the list, roles and responsibilities, is a significant product, because as people's everyday work lives (responsibilities) are modified, there will be as a natural corollary modifications in their professional relationships (roles). Furthermore, although the roles and responsibilities must be addressed in the planning phase because they will both direct and be affected by the actual implementation, this is a product that is in transition—an ever-evolving deliverable.

As the implementation moves forward and the productivity improvement begins to realize some tangible benefits, the relationship between the users, the change agents, and their emerging environment will also change. The goal at this stage of the process is to lay a foundation and establish some basic ground rules. You would realize no benefit from a comprehensive document, such as a charter or service agreement. You just need to supply a deliverable with some substance that will be flexible enough to accommodate the new environment.

Figure 8–4 contains the logical implementation plan that we developed during the planning phase when we were implementing Excelerator in our organization. This diagram depicted the relationship between my group and the other groups, which were organized according to functional responsibility (system test, designers, etc). The project team developed a proposal that identified who would be responsible for individual versions of each system as they progressed through the development life cycle. As this particular productivity improvement flourished, the roles and responsibilities altered somewhat and became defined in greater detail; however, the fundamental tenets set forth and illustrated in Figure 8–4 held true for years.

The final item on our list may be of minor significance for some implementations or may not even be appropriate for others. For example, if you are incorporating a new word processor into your department, it is doubtful that you would need to invest a lot of time and energy into developing and documenting change control and version control. On the other hand, in the Excelerator example described above, we did indeed establish version control and change control.

In fact, the change control was initiated by a member of the project team. I and the rest of my group were so involved with producing the detailed plans and gearing up for the actual implementation that although we had considered version control, we had never given a single thought to change control. One day a project team member, who happened to be a peer and friend, stopped by my office and announced the need for change control. I immediately agreed. We drafted a proposal, presented it to the team, and after minor modification documented a procedure that basically was never altered. Some things worth noting about this story are as follows:

- The presence and benefit of the informal network in action
- Receptivity of the main missionary to the innovations of disciples

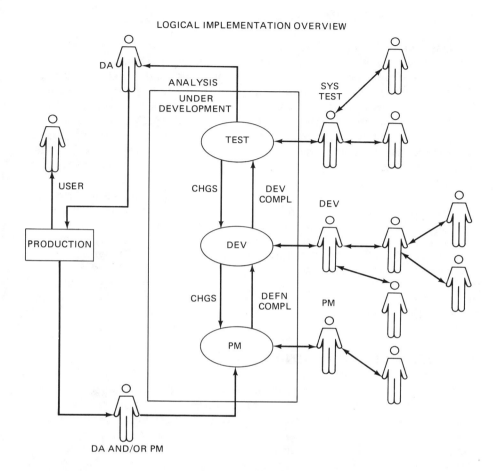

Figure 8–4 Roles and responsibilities of each group in the organization indicates which group will incorporate changes at any phase of the software development life cycle.

- Utilization of the different perspective of a team member by the team leader
- Development of a draft proposal through a cooperative effort
- Open-minded attitude of proposers to the ideas of other team members
- Production of a deliverable that truly stood the test of time

In general, our implementation of Excelerator was a very pleasant experience, and we will be sharing more examples in later chapters. The story related here illustrates the flavor and tone of that productivity tool's incorporation into our environment. Indeed, each individual productivity improvement really does depend on the product, the organization, the existing procedures, the expectations of users, and the complexity of the implementation.

THE MANAGEMENT PERSPECTIVE

While the interproject team is busily preparing all these handsome packages, you may find that, as was the case during the gathering information phase, your management may express impatience. In the previous phase we advised that you should insist and even fight if necessary to ensure you had the planning time. During this phase, you are in a more favorable position because it is possible to accede to their demands without relinquishing anything that you need to accomplish your objectives. What your management is searching for and needs to satisfy *their* management is results. Fortunately, you can provide concrete and tangible deliverables such as the Gantt charts (and numerous associated reports upon request), standards, and roles and responsibilities, to name but a few.

Since the very fiber of every manager's daily life consists of plans and reports, they should be able to relate quite nicely to the products your team is developing. In fact, even before the team develops its first deliverable, you will be able to provide them with agendas for and minutes from each project team meeting. Thus, they will not only be informed of your activities and progress, but also be reassured that resources are not being wasted. You should have no trouble politely requesting and insisting upon several months for this phase. Remember, though, even if you have an option to do so, do not get caught up here for too long. Keep the process moving.

OPTIMIZATION OF OPPORTUNITIES

In term of progress there are undoubtedly many ways that you can get stuck, and we will continue to make you aware of the perils as well as offering techniques to avoid hazards. Intrinsic to our philosophy for changing your environment is the concept of optimizing situations and resources and even the possibility of generating some opportunities of your own. For example, we believe you can direct the implementation in a manner that will result in a series of successes. Searching for instances with high probability of success and then actualizing them has the obvious benefit of gaining tremendous support from management and the user community. We mentioned this idea in the previous phase during our discussion of setting a course in the data management example. In that case, we explained the various reasons that we chose to begin our phased implementation with the interfaces. When you are directing your project team to develop a schedule of activities, you must search for similar opportunities.

Suppose you are implementing Excelerator and you know a systems analyst who is an expert in structured systems analysis, and who has expressed tremendous interest in trying an automated tool for system definition and design. You are also aware he works on a new project that is about to begin development. There may be many other options available to you for the initial implementation, but unless you get a management directive to do otherwise, you should seriously consider beginning with this one. Your potential user is enthusiastic and well trained, and the timing for his project is optimal. You will have many similar opportunities throughout the change process; be open to them and act on as many of them as possible.

There is another subtle facet to the selection of which activities you schedule first. We have just stressed the fact that you must cast about for successes. But you must also consider just as carefully the speed of delivery. In other words, you may be presented with several options, each with a high probability of success. One can be delivered in a few months, while the other may take a year. It may even be true that the one that will require a year is the most visible project in your organization. Take, for example, the enthusiastic and well-trained systems analyst described above. Maybe his project's plan has the first release scheduled for 2 years from now. However attractive an option may be, if it has a time frame as long as this, you cannot afford to select it. Remember the major initial reservation on the part of management and users alike: there was no immediate personal relief for any existing problem.

Even though you have carefully chosen the target area as well as the tool, you have successfully sold your management and users, and you have begun your implementation prudently by gathering information and planning, you cannot ever afford to lose sight of the fact that this is still a tomorrow proposition. The sooner that you can make tomorrow today (even with one intermediate deliverable), that is the moment when the hardest task of your implementation will be accomplished. Indeed, the remainder of the change process will be finishing the implementation, which will surely require years. However, your chances of success will be excellent.

SUMMARY

- Due to the time involved and the long-range ramifications, you must provide strategic and tactical plans as well as a detailed implementation plan.
- The plans will be developed by the interproject team; this is the first arena in which you may well face political opposition.
- To avoid group gropes you must begin the preparation of every deliverable with a draft document supplied by your group.
- Some of the most common outputs of this phase are Gantt charts, dependency diagrams, standards, and naming conventions.
- In order to keep the change process progressing, you must search for successes that will result in speedy delivery.

9

Standards and Naming Conventions

Nothing stirs up absolute boredom in the hearts of data processing professionals like the very mention of the word *standards*. There have been enough words written on the subject to outnumber *War and Peace* in terms of sheer volume. However, there is no use denying that without them, there is absolutely no hope for improving productivity; all you will accomplish is to mechanize your confusion faster.

WHY STANDARDIZE?

There are several fundamental reasons why an organization truly requires standards and naming conventions. The primary reason is inherent in the manner in which almost all systems are developed; except in very rare instances, none of us develop systems alone, and thus all the work we perform is just a portion of the whole. A typical scenario might be the development of a new payroll system and some of the work breakdown might be as follows: One group might be responsible for the user interface which will be used in the business office, while another is defining, designing, and implementing the employee database; still another group will be working on the subsystem that will format and produce the paychecks. It is clear there is a reason for the entire staff of each group to adopt common methodologies and naming conventions for the development of the payroll system. It would not make any sense if the user interface defined employee as a 4 character login id, the database group defined it as a 7 digit randomly generated number, and the paycheck group used the 9 digit social security number. But in our scenario that is exactly what did happen; unfortunately, as we all know from experience this does not occur all that infrequently (see Figure 9–1a).

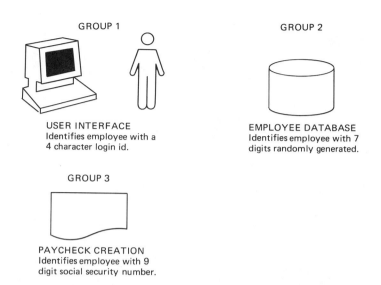

GROUP 1

USER INTERFACE
Identifies employee with a
4 character login id.

GROUP 2

EMPLOYEE DATABASE
Identifies employee with 7
digits randomly generated.

GROUP 3

PAYCHECK CREATION
Identifies employee with 9
digit social security number.

Figure 9–1a Development of the new payroll system evolved without the benefit of standards.

Let's expand our example further, because the impact of not establishing naming conventions will extend beyond the payroll system. Across the hall is a group that is developing an on-line work scheduling system for the service centers. It so happens that this system will have a batch interface to the database to provide data about exception time reporting. The work scheduling system plans to identify employees by first and last names.

Figure 9–1b contains a data flow diagram depicting the relationship between the work scheduling system and the three subsystems of the payroll system. Let's imagine how the development story might unfold. At some point during the software development life cycle, the problem will become glaringly apparent. If the collective individuals are fortunate, this will occur early in the process, possibly during a design walk through. If they are very unlucky, the inconsistency will be detected during system test, and many people will work substantial and unpleasant overtime.

The solution may take the form of conversion programs that translate one form of employee id to another. Figure 9–1c graphically depicts the complexity of the situation due to lack of standards. After the systems have gone into production, since there will be multiple translation tables, there will be multiple occurrences of inaccurate data. People's paychecks will be incorrect much more often than if there had been a common identifier. Furthermore, since there are differences in length and data type, and even variations in the meaning of employee data field, there will be ongoing and increasing problems for the systems analysts who will maintain and enhance these systems. The bottom line is that if data is representing the same thing, it must have the same name, length, storage type, and meaning.

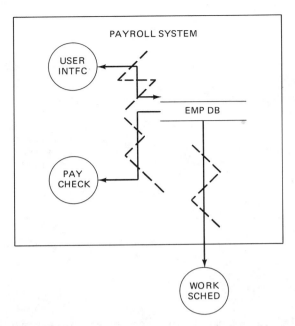

Figure 9–1b Incompatible batch interface compounds the problems of the new payroll system.

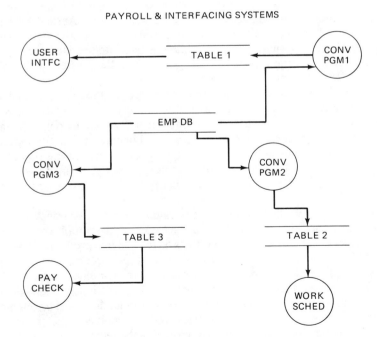

Figure 9–1c The solution imposed results in an unnecesarily complex environment.

All the problems described in this scenario relate to the data side of development, but the problems are exactly the same for the functional side. It would not facilitate a system's development if the same process depicted on two different data flow diagrams had two different names or was even represented by two different icons. Compare Figures 9–2a and 9–2b, and consider the probability of an individual recognizing that CRU and Master File Refresh represent exactly the same function. Just as in the data example, the problems were caused because the same thing (the employee record update process) was represented by different names as well as different shapes. In this case, the confusion could have been averted by a combination of a standard methodology and naming conventions.

Let's summarize the primary purpose of establishing standards and naming conventions:

- The manner in which systems are developed requires that we share information as we proceed.
- It is much easier to share information that represents the same thing if it always has the same name.
- This requirement is true for both the data and functional sides of development.
- If we do not abide by this principle, the progress of development will be slower and personally painful.
- The maintenance of systems will also be more difficult and painful.

CLASSIFICATION FACILITATES ANALYSIS

Once you have utilized standards for the purpose of identification, the second benefit of establishing these standards can be understood. For thousands of years, human beings have utilized the principle of classification to enable them to better understand their environment. Classes allow us to subset information, and this subsetting makes the information more manageable and thus easier to understand. If you set the naming conventions with intelligent foresight, you can build classes of whatever it is you are naming, and then you can analyze the subsets much more easily.

How to apply the concept of classification may not be obvious, so let's look at a few examples. Suppose you set a convention that all employee data will begin with the letter e, all customer data will begin with the letter c, and so on. After all the data has been defined and named, you can gather data from all the systems your organization supports by the classes (employee, customer, etc.). Then you can begin analyzing and identifying redundancy within and across systems. Of course, you can always search for, analyze, and identify redundancies without classes and subsetting. However, considering the quantity, the analysis would be substantially more complex and dramatically slower if you were dealing with all the data in your organization's systems at one time.

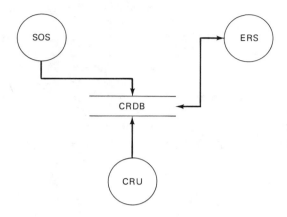

Figure 9–2a CRU (Customer Record Update) performs nightly updates to the CRDB (Customer Record Data Base).

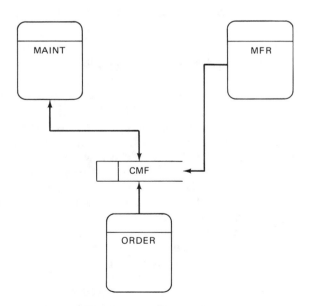

Figure 9–2b   MFR (Master File Refresh) also performs nightly updates to the CMF (Customer Master File).

You can provide yourself with similar opportunities on the functional side. For example, you might establish the following convention: Each process will begin with the first alphabetic of the system of which it is a part. This alphabetic will be followed by a dash (—) and then there will be a character that represents its function, such as u for update, a for add, and d for delete. The final component of the process name will be an English name, such as *employee record*. In our system development scenario, this convention might translate to the following:

P-A-Employee__Record

W-A-Employee__Record

where the P represents the payroll system, the W represents the work scheduling system, and the A represents the add function. The advantage in this case is that possible common functionality across systems can be identified. These potentially redundant functions can be analyzed with the objective of developing reusable code. Upon examination, it may be clear that although these functions are not identical in the two systems, there are opportunities for the two systems to use some of the same routines.

On the other hand, you may determine that the functionality is exactly the same, and then you might prefix the process with a C for common. Once all the common functions are identified and the corresponding processes are tagged with a C, it becomes possible to begin reusing code. Specifically, whenever a new system is being designed, the analysts can review all the processes that begin with a C which represents all the existing common code. It would have been very difficult for these development opportunities to become apparent without subsetting via classification and the subsequent analysis.

Before we proceed to the next reason we need standards and naming conventions, let's summarize our observations about reason two:

- Human beings use classification to help make sense of their environment.
- Intelligent planning during the establishment of naming conventions allows you to classify functionality and data.
- The components of your systems will be subsetted and so you can search for opportunities to eliminate redundancy.

COMMON LANGUAGE AS A LEGACY

The third and final reason we will offer to convince you of the importance of establishing standards and naming conventions has to do with the people. If there is a common understanding of what is meant by employee, customer, update, delete, and so on, then it is much more likely that people will be able to communicate effectively on a given project. Moreover, you have also selected a common set of methodologies and techniques, for the life cycle, structured systems analysis, and data modeling. The sum total of the commonalty can be favorably compared to a language, where the naming conventions are the vocabulary and the methodologies are the syntax. Indeed, this "common language" will extend beyond individual projects and will afford benefits across projects as well as time. In other words, people on different projects will be able to understand each other better. In addition, the next project will begin with the rich inheritance of this common language. The benefits can be summarized as follows:

- Common names and standard methodologies enable people to communicate more effectively.
- People can transition to other projects more easily.
- The task of assimilating projects will be simplified for people new to the organization.
- Certain tasks performed as part of the development process may not have to be redone.

NEGATIVE ATTITUDES TOWARD STANDARDS

Given that there are such substantial benefits to be realized by utilizing standards and naming conventions, we must now seriously question the negative attitude most of us have when they are even mentioned. A great deal of our abhorrence is related to creativity, because there has always been an emphasis in data processing on the creative aspects. In fact, one of the attractions the profession holds for many of us is the almost infinite diversity; there is so much to learn and the technology is constantly changing. We may be frequently overworked, tired and behind schedule, but we are seldom bored. Since we appreciate and even thrive on a high degree of creativity, we do not view the prospect of conforming to standards with enthusiasm.

A more tangible reason for our resentment is associated with the burden that adhering to standards represents. We are (as has been stated many times) very busy, and incorporating the standard names and complying with the rules of the methodologies is perceived as one more burden. These extra steps require substantial work during all phases of development, and we are already working more than full time. Moreover, these steps are not even interesting, but tend to be somewhat repetitious and even tedious. A corollary to this reason for resistance is the possibility that the standards may be in opposition to names or methodologies that already exist. If this is the situation, then not only are we dealing with "extra" work, but we are dealing with the possibility of "redoing" work that in our minds is already complete.

The last theory we will propose for resistance to standards has to do with negative connotations of authority. None of us is thrilled when an "authority" enters the scene and suggests numerous ways for us to improve our current situation. We are even less happy when the methods proposed by this self-proclaimed authority require a lot of work on our part. In general, it is also unclear to us what advantage we will gain after all this extra and tedious work has been completed.

Before we proceed with advice and suggestions on the subject, let's recap the traditional causes for resistance:

- Data processing professionals take pride in their creativity, and thus conforming to standards is offensive to them.
- Adhering to standards entails substantial extra work on the part of already overworked people.
- Since names and methodologies may already exist, the extra work may take the form of redoing work already completed.
- We resent the possibility of some authority arbitrarily imposing standards.

ROLE OF THE PROJECT TEAM

It would seem indisputable that judicious planning and incorporation of standards and naming conventions are essential to any data processing effort. Moreover, in spite of all the problems you will encounter, it is in fact possible to establish them and encourage their use. There are four fundamental commandments to which you must adhere if you want to establish standards that are robust enough to endure and humane enough to be used. First, you must formulate both standards and naming conventions within the framework of the project team. Since we have been advising you to prepare all deliverables in draft form and then approach the team for input, this may seem like a contradiction. However, your group is simply not in a position to make determinations that will have profound ramifications for everyone else; they simply do not have enough insight to arrive at even a draft document that is appropriate.

On the other hand, we are not suggesting that you begin this particular project team meeting without having given some thought to the subject; you should have some idea with which to start the discussion. But it is paramount that you be even more open-minded than usual when this topic is addressed. The objective is to poll the individual perspectives of the various team members because they represent the diverse functions of the development life cycle. The deliverable that results will be a collection of their expertise, and thus should be hardier than one devised by any single group.

During our implementation of Excelerator, we had a particularly grueling meeting to develop the naming convention we would use for elements. At that project team meeting we had many different aspects of data processing represented; in attendance were planners, systems analysts, programmers, system testers, and a data dictionary expert. In addition, there were several team members with extremely strong personalities and very definite opinions. It was not a very pleasant morning. However, time does tend to dim pain, and what I am left with in terms of the experience is the fact that we arrived at a superb naming convention.

The morning began with the data dictionary expert, Joe, stating unequivocally that the only way to ensure the integrity of the Excelerator dictionary was to utilize a four-digit number that is randomly generated for the element name. Before the words were fully uttered, the systems analyst, Betty, replied that there was no possibility that numeric element names could be used when dealing with users. Joe reemphasized his point with the following example:

Suppose the element we are trying to describe is type of equipment...
According to Joe's suggestion the name given to type of equipment might be:

6357

According to Betty's request for an English name, any of the possibilities listed below might be used:

type of equipment
type of equip
type of eqpt
equipment type
equip type
eqpt type

Moreover, the names listed above are but a few of the ones that individual people might develop.

Betty became increasingly upset, and claimed she could not live with numbers. Then she threw out the ultimate threat; she was just going to have to report all this to her supervisor, since we obviously did not want her input. Joe became more adamant about uniqueness and data dictionary research studies. The rest of the team became quiet and noticeably distressed. We were all subjected to this torture for what seemed an eternity. Other team members made tentative suggestions, such as why not use the name marketing has officially adopted since its system is the origin for most of our data?

The outcome was the following standard for naming elements in our Excelerator dictionary:

For each logical data element that served a unique business function, there would be a randomly generated four-digit number.
Appended to that number would be a dash '-', followed by the English name that was most commonly used.
There would be no white space (blanks) embedded in names with more than one word. The words would be separated by underscores '__'.
There would be no lowercase letters; everything would be capitalized.
An example might be: 6357-EQUIPMENT__TYPE

One of the lessons I learned from this experience is that even under adverse conditions, it is possible to arrive at a compromise. In fact, the convention served so many diverse requirements that it survived many years. Let's examine the requirements that were met by the standard. The need for uniqueness dictated by data dictionary practices was satisfied by the randomly generated four-digit prefix. Four digits were selected as the number required, because that will allow for 9,999 distinct elements. Since this count does not include the hundreds of aliases we all apply regularly to our data names, in theory the 9,999 should fully describe the data environment for any business. The human factors side of data processing was addressed by appending a common business name.

The selection of the English name was left open on an element by element basis and was to be supplied to our group at the time a request for a new element was initiated. This is a fact that is well worth noting: As change agents, we never assumed we had any particular insight for setting standards or establishing naming conventions. Throughout the entire process, we remained open to suggestions from our users, and wherever possible we utilized whatever standards they recommended. Our philosophy was that if it was working for or desired by even one group, and we had no reason to believe it would adversely affect any other group, we would abide by the suggestion.

PROVIDE OPPORTUNITIES, NOT EDICTS

This philosophy harks back to the orientation of the change group we discussed earlier; the people must understand that this is a service group and thus must make every attempt to cooperate. On the other hand, you must ensure that by honoring an individual user's request, there are no negative implications for other groups. If other users cannot abide by the convention or two different users propose contradictory standards, then you as the leader must make the decision. In either situation, you cannot cooperate and you must be prepared for a confrontation if necessary. Do not forget that you have been given the job of implementing the change, and thus you also have the authority to mandate solutions when obliged by circumstances.

In Chapter 3 we discussed the inappropriateness of a centralized group performing the evaluation of the tool or technique. However, we did indicate that there is a very important role for these centralized groups in terms of coordination. In the area of standards, the role of centralized coordination is something you cannot afford to ignore. Optimally there will be available for your use a document that provides corporate guidelines for establishing standards and naming conventions that have already been defined. We stress the word guidelines because if the corporate policy extends beyond that, then there is a fundamental problem.

Similar to our view about who performs product evaluation, we are also firmly convinced that the people who will be utilizing the productivity product should also set the standards. They will be the ones who have to live with the results of the decisions, and so it is perfectly clear that they should make the decisions. On the other hand, no one wants a situation where every group is establishing separate and distinct standards. Remember our example about the two departments that were both developing a standard employee id. In that case, a disaster was averted by the involvement of the corporate group. The ideal situation occurs when there is flexibility for each individual organization within a framework of centralized guidelines.

When we were establishing the conventions for element names described above, we were not networked into our corporate standards group. It was over a year later, when we were finishing our implementation, that we began to exchange information with them. We were quite fortunate, because their policy matched our own and thus they were extremely flexible. They had a corporate data catalog that contained the official names of the data elements deemed to be critical to the corporation. Their only request to local groups such as ours was that we retain the ability in our dictionary to map their name to our own.

We added an "ideal" name to our element naming conventions, and that name was the official corporate one. We also established a guideline that this ideal name would be our goal, and we recommended that whenever programmers were modifying or enhancing code that contained names which were aliases for this one, they should consider changing all occurrences to the ideal name. Figure 9–3 displays the relationships between the dictionaries and the software.

We assessed possible areas for improvement within the actual software itself, but we were appreciative of the tremendous amount of work that would be

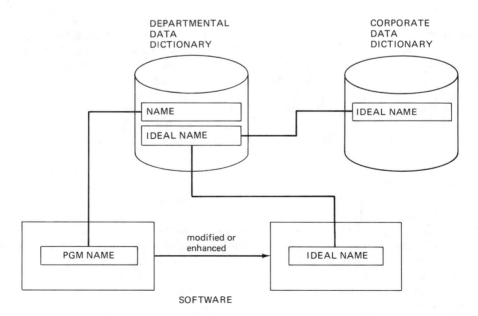

Figure 9–3 Through the use of appropriate naming conventions, it is possible to maintain relationships between dictionaries and the software itself.

involved in changing program names. There was a planner on the project team who recommended we mandate all program names be changed to this standard, but we never for a moment considered this suggestion seriously. Although well intentioned the planner did not understand the magnitude of her suggestion because she had never been a programmer. The team did realize the impact of this type of software modification not only on the programmers and on system test, but also the problems related to scheduling this into existing release plans. Moreover, we already understood a great deal about implementing productivity improvements. We knew that this type of far-reaching recommendation must be born in the project team arena, and that it must be an objective that all team members can be comfortable with. Even more important, we knew that any recommendation must be something that had a chance of success. Since not one of those ingredients was present, all we did was to point out an opportunity. We did not present an unreasonable edict for the people who would have to do the actual work. This type of interaction substantially increased our credibility and greatly enhanced our implementation.

Let's pause and relate this case study to some of the causes of resistance described in the beginning of the chapter:

- We as the change agents did not impose seemingly arbitrary naming conventions on our users.
- The naming conventions we ultimately applied represented the collective input of many diverse groups (including corporate and programming).
- We did not attempt to exert any undue authority on any of the people who would have to perform the work.
- We did not suggest that anyone should redo any work that had been completed.
- We did recommend that the standards be incorporated whenever there might be opportunities in the future to do so without disruption.
- By conducting the change process in this manner, we gained substantial credibility.

BUILD ON EXISTING STANDARDS

The second fundamental commandment for setting standards is never to disregard a naming convention that already exists. If people have consciously or unconsciously established even something as modest as a pattern for naming any type of item (files, records, user ids, processes, etc.), it behooves you to incorporate the pattern in your standards. There are several reasons why you should defer to any prior work in this area. The first one is that you have no reason to believe you have any more talent for evolving conventions than anyone else. Therefore, based on your commitment to cooperation, it will be helpful to use anything already developed.

These reasons can also be directly related to the resistance issues discussed earlier in the chapter. This type of accommodation avoids the change agents being viewed as self-proclaimed authorities; this is often the negative perception of people trying to establish standards. You will also gain credibility because you will not precipitate extra work, nor will you cause any work that has been done to be redone. What you will do is to utilize names, standards, and even patterns that are already in use. This creative establishment of standards will contribute to what we call "creating the proper environment" in which change can take place.

In our Excelerator implementation, we were able to follow some of this advice in connection to naming conventions for interface records, as the following tale illustrates. It was during the planning period, and we had already decided that prior to utilization of the tool by the existing maintenance systems, we would load all their interface records and elements into the dictionary. Since we had already set an element naming convention (during the infamous meeting described above), we were prepared to set some standards for the record names as well. What occurred, however, was that upon examination of the names that were currently being utilized for both the physical and logical views of the systems, we discovered a definite pattern. Every record began with two alphabetic characters: the first character was the first letter of the sending system, and the second character was the first letter of the receiving system. In other words, all the records from Service Order System (SOS) to Equipment Repair System (ERS) began with SE. The third and fourth characters were numeric, and it turned out that their combination indicated the type of record. For example, any record that had 47 as the third and fourth characters contained equipment information. Thus SE47 was the record sent from the Service Order System; the destination was the Equipment Repair System; and the information on the record was about equipment (see Figure 9–4).

We adopted that particular naming convention without the slightest modification or hesitation. There was even one interface that did not follow this pattern, and for some reason (lost to modern history) began with an alphabetic character different from the sending system. We debated about whether to change the name of the records or to diverge from the convention. We decided to proceed with the actual record name, even though it would break newly set precedent. Our reasoning had, once again, to do with the issues of resistance and disruption. As we have mentioned previously, there will be a tendency for people to view the change agents as disruptive, but we do not accept that this negative view is inevitable. Bearing in mind our objective of avoiding this view and hence minimizing resistance, we carefully considered our options. Everyone in the organization was used to the existing record names, so we balanced the pros and cons of adhering strictly to conventions against allowing our users to be comfortable. This was, in reality, not even a slightly difficult decision for the team to reach, and to my knowledge only one individual ever questioned why that set of records was named differently.

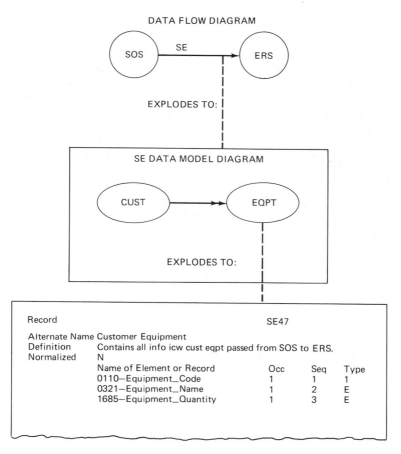

Figure 9–4 On the data flow diagram the SE interface between SOS and ERS explodes to the SE data model diagram where the entity, eqpt. explodes to the SE47 record.

ENFORCING STANDARDS

The third commandment in reality addresses the difficulties associated with enforcing standards once they have been established. None of us has a desire to play the role of police officer, and yet that is frequently the role people adopt after they have set standards. It is a fact that the difficulties you encounter when you are establishing standards can be negligible compared to the difficulties you can face trying to enforce them. Notice that we used the word <u>can</u>, because it is our belief that if you utilize the techniques we have described, you will not have too much trouble. Because you will be establishing your conventions from within the team arena, you will listen effectively to team members and utilize the benefits of their expertise. You will also capitalize on any work already accomplished. In addition, you will arrange things so that it will be easy for your users to adhere to the standards. This ease of use is the heart of the third commandment.

The most dramatic application of ease of use involves the creation of templates. A friend of mine worked for a corporation whose upper management had wholeheartedly adopted a life cycle methodology. When the company became committed to the need for a project planning and tracking tool, he was given the responsibility for implementing Project Workbench. He immediately created a template that contained all the phases and activities proscribed by the methodology. (Figure 9–5 is a sample, which for the sake of simplicity contains phases only.) Whenever a project manager was ready to begin using PW, he supplied that person with the template. Before the manager even began planning the project, considerable work had been completed. It is not hard to believe that in this case not only was there a high rate of adherence to the standards, but there was also an impressive display of consistency from project to project.

PROJECT: Project_Life_Cycle_Template

Project_Life_Cycle_Template	Da	Who	28	January 1988				February 1988				
				4	11	18	25	1	8	15	22	29
Business Problem				•	•	•	•	•	•	•	•	•
Feasibility				•	•	•	•	•	•	•	•	•
User Requirements				•	•	•	•	•	•	•	•	•
System Definition				•	•	•	•	•	•	•	•	•
Logical Design				•	•	•	•	•	•	•	•	•
Physical Design				•	•	•	•	•	•	•	•	•
System Build				•	•	•	•	•	•	•	•	•
Unit Test				•	•	•	•	•	•	•	•	•
System Test				•	•	•	•	•	•	•	•	•
User Acceptance Test				•	•	•	•	•	•	•	•	•
Implementation				•	•	•	•	•	•	•	•	•
Post Implement Review				•	•	•	•	•	•	•	•	•

Figure 9–5.   Templates do not enforce standards, but rather encourage adherence by reducing the work effort.

NEVER SET A STANDARD BEFORE ITS TIME

The fourth and final commandment is simply never to set a standard before its time. Keep in mind that the purpose of any standard is to streamline life; it should never impose additional burdens on already harassed users. If what is being done with the tool or technique during any phase of the change process does not warrant a specific standard, wait. Not only does it avoid unnecessarily burdening your users, but it saves you, your group, and the project team time and effort that can be gainfully employed in a more critical area.

If you find yourself with the luxury of some not too terribly overworked people, do not be tempted to establish conventions and save them for the right time. You will discover that the right time may never come. As the change process progresses, the environment will begin to evolve, and the premature standards may no longer apply.

A CASE STUDY

Our Excelerator implementation was, on the whole, a very pleasant experience. The way we developed our standards was characteristic of the entire productivity improvement (even the grueling meeting takes on a rosy hue as the years pass). We established some basic and minimal standards during the planning phase, as follows:

- Selection of methodologies to be followed in order to avoid having one project use Gane & Sarson while another used Yourdon.
- Adoption of element naming conventions.
- Selection of ideal element names, which would be the one name we would use in all future programs in order to provide consistency in the physical systems.
- Adoption of record naming conventions.
- Adoption of coding scheme to accommodate functional aspects of development (as described in the payroll example).

What happened next was that at various points in the implementation we were approached by users who requested additional standards, procedures, etc. In the last chapter, we shared the story of how change control was user-initiated and was included toward the end of the planning phase. Another occurrence of this type of user-initiated establishment of conventions is related to version control. During the planning phase, we had provided some ground rules for handling the versions of each system as they moved through the release cycle. However, these rules only covered the roles and responsibilities that would exist between my group and the users. Many months later, when we were finishing our implementation, our most sophisticated user recommended that we include version as part of our element, record, and process naming conventions. The proposal was to append a version number to each element, record, or process that was being added or modified at any given time. Using the examples given earlier, if SOS was changing the equipment type element's length on the SE47 record in their 1.7 release, the following names would be used:

SE47__1.7   for the record
6357-EQUIPMENT__TYPE__1.7   for the element
S-U-WORK__ORDER__1.7   for the process

When the SOS 1.7 release went into production, the __1.7 would be dropped as a suffix in the name of the record, element, and process. Since at that phase there was no longer an active interproject team, we socialized this suggestion with a number of other project managers to obtain a preliminary readout, and then we published a draft form for comment to our user community.

We did not start our implementation by presenting a road map with predetermined routes all laid out for the course of the change process. Instead, we were open to everyone's recommendations for the implementation of our productivity improvement. In the early stages, this easy method of interaction between ourselves and at least some of our users about standards and conventions already indicated some measure of success. At least we were laying the foundation for what we term "the proper environment." There was no doubt that we had established a certain degree of credibility: They believed we were sincere about acting in their best interests because we were willing to take our cues from them. Never did we dictate how things were going to be done or the correct name for anything, although we were not afraid to make decisions and provide needed leadership. Over the course of the implementation, as this free exchange of ideas increased, so did the environment of trust and confidence, which without a doubt resulted not only in a major success story, but also a nontraumatic path to arrive there.

SUMMARY

- Since many people develop a system, we need to share information. Standards afford a consistency that facilitates this sharing.
- Naming conventions enable us to classify information, which provides a capability to subset, analyze, and identify redundant data and functionality.
- We resent standards because we are creative as well as overworked, and they are often arbitrarily imposed by self-proclaimed authorities.
- Standards must be established by project team members who represent the diverse functions of the development lifecycle. Then the resultant deliverable will be hardy enough to stand the test of time.
- Standards should be easy to use, capitalize on existing naming conventions, and must never be established until users deem there is a need for them.

10

Implementing Change

We have finally arrived at the pivotal point of the entire change process; the previous phases have been essentially a preparation for this, and the subsequent phases will consist of the lengthy and sometimes monotonous tasks of finishing up. This is the phase during which you will travel across the bridge from the familiar, comfortable, and less than optimal world of today and take the first tenuous steps into the modern and interesting environment you have envisioned. It is no accident that we use the expression "first tenuous steps," because the manner in which change is effected is a series of small, steady steps.

There will be no overnight miraculous and dramatic improvement in productivity, but rather a gradual and sometimes almost imperceptible acceptance and adjustment on the part of your users. Finally one day it will be clear to users and management alike that there has been a definite change. As they reflect on this fact, it will also occur to them that this is a desirable situation and that they are proud to have been a part of it. That they have indeed been a part of the process is unquestionably true because their participation and involvement is what made it a success. As an agent of change, one of your most valuable functions in all phases is to enable your users to understand and appreciate the productivity product, and then feel comfortable enough to incorporate it into their lives.

FACING THE INSURMOUNTABLE

Up to the present, you have been assessing, selecting, evaluating, selling, listening, analyzing, and planning, all of which has allowed people many opportunities to understand and appreciate what you are doing. Now you will begin the process of actively modifying your organization. This can be an exhilarating thought, but it may also be quite overwhelming. It can be a moment of substantial self-doubt: Can I really get all those people to use Project Workbench, or can I really load all the data into the dictionary? It is understandable that the job might seem insurmountable, and because of this fact, many change agents just cannot get started. However, take heart, because we have practical and reliable techniques to share for this phase too.

First, in order to restore our confidence, let's examine the timeline provided in Figure 10–1, which provides an example of the data management implementation. Each phase is charted, along with the month and year that it was completed or slated for completion. (Please note that specific months and years are for illustrative purposes only). It is reasonable to be impressed by the fact that from the very beginning, when we were assessing the target area, up through now, when we have completed our detailed plans, only 8 months have elapsed. A great deal has been accomplished in a very short time. Moreover, there have been considerable achievements on the intangible side; many users are already converted, and the implementation proper has not even begun.

Now that you are ready to begin, your very first activity is actually to face the fact that the task is truly insurmountable! It is not possible for you and your small group to modify (or in some instances reverse) the current mode of operation of all the individuals in your organization. Nevertheless, the situation is not

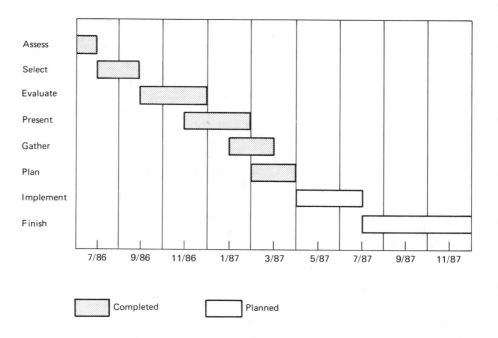

Figure 10–1   Implementing data management.

hopeless, because the way to resolve this apparent paradox is to divide the change effort into manageable chunks. You cannot change everything for everyone on day 1 of the implementation phase; you must set some reasonable limits and realistic goals. When you reflect upon the concept of manageable chunks, you will realize that many activities you performed in earlier phases were designed with this idea in mind.

Remember when we set a course of direction during the gathering information phase? We spent considerable time and effort analyzing the situation and attempting to determine which alternative had the highest probability of success. We also emphasized this concept of searching for successes during the development of the implementation plan by the project team. In addition, we stated that selecting tasks that were quite likely to succeed was not enough; the team must select intermediate deliverables that can be completed quickly. Hopefully, this is exactly what you and the project team did when you developed a schedule. Finally, given the fact that the task as a whole is insurmountable, the scope of your implementation must not be excessive at any one time.

AN APOCRYPHAL TALE

Truly, the most common mistake people make when they are attempting to improve productivity is that they undertake "too much too soon." A typical scenario might be similar to the following apocryphal tale. In our fictitious department, the situation at the start was somber indeed. Not only had the systems been defined, designed, and implemented under considerable time constraints, but the staff had recently been substantially reduced and morale was at an all-time low. (This situation should seem familiar because it does match the profile of an organization ripe for change we described in Chapter 1.)

The change agents accurately identified a need for productivity improvement and then selected multiple tools and techniques to address the situation. They followed every step of every phase to perfection and the result of the planning phase was an impressive, comprehensive, and detailed schedule of activities and tasks. During the early stages of the implementation phase, all software packages and appropriate data were loaded onto the designated PCs. Members of the user community were sent to training classes for all the tools and techniques. However, when the users attempted to resume their everyday work, some serious problems arose. Since many days were spent acquiring all the necessary training, they were behind schedule on their individual development projects. Moreover, there was almost nothing familiar about the routine in which they performed their jobs because their manual mode of operation had been replaced with the installation of the tools. While they had been exposed to interesting information, how to apply that knowledge with their new tools and techniques under severe pressure was not obvious. Our crusaders were undaunted, because they were highly skilled in all the tools and techniques, understood the functions being mechanized, and were totally committed. But they were only three in number, and there were only so many hours per day. They could help only a limited number of users. The organization's collective frustration expanded on a daily basis.

As the days went by, completing tasks on everyone's schedules (projects and productivity improvement alike) became increasingly impossible. There had been no significant progress with the implementation of any one tool or technique, and everyone (upper management, change agents, and users) was thoroughly disenchanted. This sad end to our tale was in no way inevitable, because there were several critical success factors in place: the time was right, the tool and techniques were good, there was management support, and the change agents were both competent and committed. The disaster was caused by not being selective, not setting realistic goals, not carving out a manageable chunk, and generally attempting too much too soon.

The situation was further aggravated because the change agents did not reevaluate the plan when they encountered substantial obstacles. As we all know, it is often true that carefully prepared plans are never considered after they are completed. The up-front planning is usually demanded by upper management, but the tracking and controlling often get lost in the heat of the actual implementation. The message here is that you need to develop a plan that not only accounts for the tasks to be accomplished but also allows for unforeseen problems (remember the slippage capability in PW). As you implement the change, you need to monitor the plan to ensure not only that you are on schedule, but that each task still makes sense. There is absolutely no advantage to blind adherence; you need to constantly mentally apply sanity checks.

Let's pause and attempt to distill some of the lessons we might learn from our apocryphal tale:

- The task of actually implementing the change is virtually insurmountable.
- The way to overcome this apparent obstacle is to divide the change effort into manageable chunks.
- It is not enough to develop a detailed plan: you must also check constantly during the actual implementation to ensure that you are on schedule and that each task remains relevant.
- The most common mistake people make during this phase is attempting too much too soon.

Do not delude yourself either, there are several very attractive reasons that lead change agents into this trap. The primary cause is simply ambition; the crusader has staked a tremendous amount on the success of the change. Thus it is extremely tempting to prove the worth of the mission by setting glorious goals. The flaw in this line of reasoning is that it is virtually impossible to deliver glorious results during a productivity improvement. Remember the twin objectives— search for a series of small successes (not one glorious end), and establish a set of intermediate deliverables (not the ultimate product).

MEET EACH USER ON HIS OWN GROUND

Moreover, the manageable chunk axiom is important not only for your sanity, but also because of the fundamental philosophy of effecting a cultural change. Remember the main issue is overcoming resistance, and that is equivalent to discovering the concerns and fears of your users, and then enabling them to feel comfortable with the change process. If you begin implementation by presenting them with several productivity tools and techniques, panic is the only possible result. The objective is to change one aspect of their environment at a time. When people are accustomed to that improvement, then add another tool or technique (see Figures 10–2a and 10–2b).

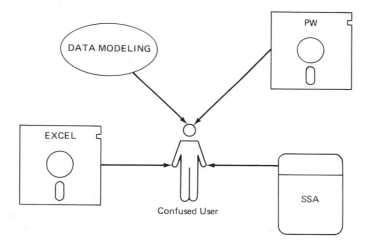

Figure 10–2a   Changing multiple aspects of the environment at once yields chaos.

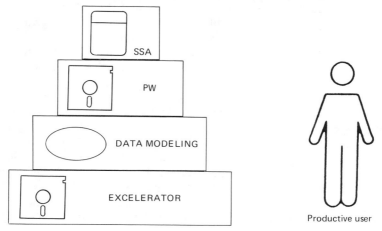

Figure 10–2b   Incremental improvements yield results.

For example, when we were in this phase of our ever so pleasant Excelerator implementation, our section was reorganized and I found myself reporting to a different boss. (This can really be a problem; we will cover unexpected reorganizations in Chapter 12.) Mercifully, this man came to us not only with an enlightened view of development, but with a high degree of belief in what we were endeavoring to achieve. However, he had begun his career in a more theoretical sector of the company and thus expressed concern that we had not planned to train all our users in structured systems analysis. His opinion (and rightly so) was that in order to maximize our benefit from the tool, people needed to become proficient in methodologies, such as those associated with data flow diagrams.

I assured my new boss that we had thought about the possibility of simultaneously training everyone to utilize Excelerator and become structured systems analysts. We had also discarded this option because we truly believed that the task of mastering either Excelerator or structured systems analysis would in itself provide a hearty challenge to our users. In reality, our user community was quite diverse in background; some people were already structured systems analysts, while others were untrained in any methodology. The course of action we adopted was one of flexibility. We did not set some artificial standard mode of utilizing the tool for our whole organization. An example of that type of approach might have been to mandate that no one was going to use the tool without first mastering the methodologies, which certainly would have placed a heavy burden on many individuals. Nor did we mandate that for the sake of consistency no one was to use the tool for any diagrams, which certainly would have set a senseless limit on the tool's initial benefit to many people. (These possibilities are not ridiculous because we have actually been in situations where this type of mentality prevails.)

The approach we did take was simply "to meet each user on her or his own ground." For example, if an individual understood structured systems analysis, we provided a copy of the tool and the minimal standards the project team had established, and then sent him off on his merry way. On the other hand, if the person was untrained in structured methods, he could still benefit from the integrated dictionary, and he could certainly understand the record layouts and screen design facility. Was he getting 100% benefit from the tool? No! Was he getting a 40% benefit from the tool? Yes! Surely a 40% benefit is better than 0; more important, he felt good about himself, the tool, and what he was doing. When he became really confident; then he could learn about the methodologies, and realize the tool's total benefit.

We had been through the change process before, so we understood the significance of making our users comfortable and the importance of incremental improvement. We knew we only had to provide intermediate deliverables quickly. Finally, we knew that if we accomplished those three objectives; then we would be permitted the time required to implement our change in its entirety. However, you must not make the mistake of underestimating the difficulty of this flexibility. It is not a simple matter constantly to assess each individual and his or her relationship to the change process; and then tailor the implementation to suit the situation. But as with other techniques you must apply during the productivity improvement, it is a skill that becomes easier to use the more you utilize it. To capture the essence of this flexibility, let's summarize the approach adopted during our Excelerator implementation:

- Effective implementation translates to manageable chunks for change agents and incremental improvements for users.
- Providing incremental improvements for users means enabling them to modify exactly one aspect of their environment at a time.
- The form that aspect will assume during the implementation will vary from user to user depending on experience levels.
- You provide that customized (and hence comfortable) situation for your users by exhibiting flexibility and meeting each user on his or her own ground.

Now that we have reviewed the fundamental tenets of actually implementing change, it is appropriate to discuss the steps that comprise it. There are very specific tasks that you will perform when you are actually implementing the productivity product: It is not merely a question of all the change agents charging about making all the users feel comfortable. After all, you and the project team spent considerable effort on the planning phase. Certainly the activities will vary considerably, depending on the product; however, there are aspects of this phase that you can depend on experiencing, regardless of what productivity improvement you are implementing. Some of these aspects are listed below:

- No matter how well you have planned, you will encounter unforeseen obstacles.
- You will utilize your informal network to surmount some of these obstacles.
- You will also capitalize on the information gathered about key people (situational leaders) to help resolve some of the difficulties.
- Dealing with these problems and the accompanying frustration is the heart of the doing phase.
- You must be prepared to deal with a renewal of discouragement and the accompanying self-doubt.
- The secret of success lies in utilizing your inherent abilities to form strategy and persist.

AN IDYLLIC TALE

We want to provide you with a realistic view of the tasks that might be involved as well as how they might be implemented. We also want to describe some specific examples of dealing with the aspects of doing listed above. To accomplish these objectives, we are going to look at a case study consisting of the real events that took place during the implementation phase of data management. We have referred to the data management implementation several times thus far; now let's examine the list below to understand the activities that took place prior to its actual implementation.

- In the past in our organization, there had been a departmental data catalog facility that had been discontinued during a major reorganization.
- The data for our systems was definitely out of control; elements had as many as three dozen known aliases in the logical views of the systems and hundreds of names in the programs.
- A definite need for data management was assessed and sold to upper management.
- A group that consisted of two people was formed for this purpose.
- There was a period during which we reawakened awareness of the value of data management in the minds of our users.
- We spent some time gathering information from our users and developed a course of direction (see Chapter 6).
- An interproject team was formed to develop:
    Phased implementation plan
    Schedule of activities
    Standards and naming conventions
    Roles and responsibilities

We, as change agents, had made a commitment never to interfere with our users' very important everyday activities or slow down their progress in any way. Therefore, we decided personally to perform all the initial data analysis and then hire some temporary clerical support to enter the data into the dictionary. The first thing we did was gather all the documentation that existed about any system for which we were providing the data management service. The documents that we collected were these:

- User requirements
- System definition
- Logical design document
- Physical design (databases)
- User guides
- Interface specifications
- Data element profiles
- Data catalog (outdated)
- Program documentation
- Data structures from the programs (e.g. COBOL data division)

The amount, type, and quality of documentation varied enormously from system to system. For example, the Service Order System (SOS) suffered from overdocumentation; every day piles of paper were delivered to each project team member. Needless to say, there were many instances of inconsistency from document to document, and the sheer quantity was overwhelming. At one time I had been a project leader of the programming staff; and I (and my boss) always promptly threw all the papers in the trash as soon as they were delivered. At the other extreme, dealing with the Equipment Repair System (ERS) was tantamount to entering the twilight zone; we were lucky to obtain encrypted paper napkins. If a system is virtually undocumented, you might infer that there had been a notable lack of definition and design. It would not surprise anyone to hear that the system was extremely error-prone and crashed on a regular basis. In fact, I was once in charge of production management of this system and was beeped once an hour for three long months.

Since we had been part of the organization for a number of years, we were in an extremely favorable position. We were familiar with many of the systems and their associated data, which facilitated our analysis, as well as greatly aiding our credibility. Moreover, we knew many of our users and hence were starting from a position of trust and confidence. The relevance of these two facts has been noted in previous chapters, and it certainly was true in this case. We understood the modality of the organization—who to ask for help or information, who to avoid. Another way of framing this is to state that we were acquainted with the informal organization and in general understood how to get things done quickly and without fuss. All these facts enabled us to perform the analysis speedily and without distraction to our users.

Over the course of the next several weeks, while the clerks entered the data into our dictionary, Sally and I prepared all the data model diagrams that were required to represent the organization's data. This was a bottom-up view of the data architecture as it currently existed, and the data was not normalized. We had elected to provide the diagrams personally so that we could ensure a consistent foundation for all future data work in the organization. Does this sound idyllic? Of course, and to be honest, this was not exactly how the implementation proceeded. What did happen was that at every step of the way we were met by concrete and substantial impediments. We constantly had to replan the change process while simultaneously persisting in our efforts to do the job. During the course of the implementation, it sometimes seemed that we no longer had a plan.

THE REAL STORY

When we began to gather the documentation, we encountered our first stumbling block. This obstacle took the form of noncooperation on the part of our users. Some of this resistance was unintentional; they were just too busy to stop and search for outdated and useless documentation, so they promised to get back to us. Sometimes they did and sometimes they forgot, but almost never was the information provided speedily. We addressed this problem in a simple and straightforward manner; we proceeded with sensitivity and perception, and we gently persisted.

For example, if they were about to hand a release over to system test in a few days, we waited until they were not so busy. Since we were extremely courteous and we had already established friendly relations with most of these people, our patience was usually rewarded, and after a few gentle reminders we received what we needed. If not, we offered to come over (at their convenience), and help search for the material.

Occasionally we met with political barriers. The project manager of SOS was one of the less cooperative members of our interproject team and continued in that role during this phase. No matter how simple our request was, it presented a problem for him and he took forever to provide the document. We handled this resistance in exactly the same manner as we handled the behavior of our busy friends. We timed our requests opportunely, we were patient, and we politely persisted. Once when we simply could not obtain the necessary document, we went to one of his staff members, who was a friend of ours. After we had the document in hand, I wrote a laudatory memo to my boss commending the interest and cooperation of this man and his group, despite their heavy workload. I carbon-copied the SOS project manager, who found it very difficult to complain about us after a public display of praise about him and his people.

When we approached the ERS group, they stated unequivocally that our request was impossible because all that existed was the software itself. We sweetly reminded them that we had both written many programs in our time and we would be delighted if they would just provide us with copies of the COBOL data division, the PL/1 structures, etc. Then Sally helped them retrieve the copylib members so it required less than one hour of time from one programmer.

The morning the temporary clerks were scheduled to arrive for their first day at work, my boss informed us that he had arranged for us to give a status report to upper management. There was no possibility of rescheduling the status report, nor was there any benefit to delaying the start date of the clerks. We squelched any stirring of disquiet and hastily prepared the status report. Then we placed on the clerks' desks two manuals that described the editor they would be using, along with a note telling them to start reading and practicing. (Happily, the meeting lasted only two hours, so this turned out not to be a major conflict.)

As we progressed with the data load, it became apparent that one of the clerks was less than useless. Worse than the fact that she could not cope with the assignment was the fact she continually interrupted the other clerk for help. After a brief hesitation, we terminated her services at the end of the first week. Our reasoning was that if we had to prepare the information for her in great detail, her involvement did not add any benefit, and we could not afford any extra work when we had such a demanding schedule. Moreover, we were not dealing with one of our staff members to whom we owed an obligation as a supervisor. (We did after all have our more ruthless moments.) We hired another temporary clerk who seemed even less competent than the one we had just dismissed, so Sally dismissed him while I negotiated with our boss. I told him that the one clerk was so superior we did not want to hire another one, but preferred to keep him twice as long. With his agreement, we chewed our fingernails as PW automatically recalculated our schedule and the critical path on our dependency diagram. We heaved gigantic sighs of relief when it became clear we had built enough slippage into our schedule to still have a chance at meeting our commitments.

Do we sound like a couple of superwomen who were on top of every situation? Well, it surely did not feel that way. It would be a conservative estimate to say that we were extremely discouraged at least half of the time. It was so hard to believe that the small portion of data that comprised phase 1 could possibly make a significant contribution to productivity. Indeed, there were many days when it seemed doubtful that we would be able to deliver even that small piece. But in spite of our doubts, we persisted. Actually, we did not give serious thought to any other option; we still believed as fervently as ever. Moreover, we had laid our collective careers on the line to upper management. Finally (and perhaps most important) it would have been mortifying to face our users after the marketing blitz, if we just gave up. Our only choice was to continue.

As soon as we had any portion of the work completed, we distributed it to all the first-line managers for review and sign off. This policy served multiple purposes. The political reason was to protect ourselves from repercussions later on in the change process. For example, it is not unheard of for people to suddenly emerge, months into the implementation, from their own personal crises with loud lamentations that they had not the slightest idea about what was happening. However, if you distribute results and ask for comments, suggestions, and questions by a specific date, the lamentations are much less impressive to upper management. Another benefit that we gained from this procedure was that the quality of the information was vastly improved. Each manager parceled out the in-

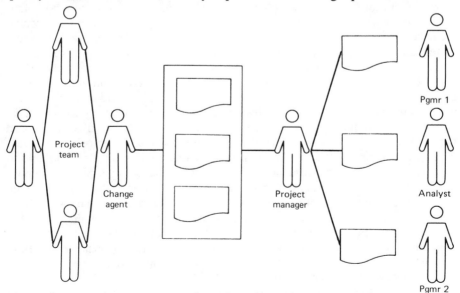

Figure 10–3 By soliciting the input of many people, the change process became an organizational effort.

formation that we had distributed to subject matter experts. The result was that the information was reviewed several times, and in addition was reviewed by the very people in the organization who knew it best.

The third benefit related to the process of increasing the number of people who buy in to the productivity improvement. This one had not even occurred to us, and yet it turned out to be the most significant of all. This involvement of such a large proportion of our organization resulted in a quality product that belonged, in fact, to the entire organization. In other words, the dictionary was not a product developed by my group and offered to the other groups; by virtue of the extensive participation, it became everyone's product (see Figure 10–3).

OFFICIAL ACCEPTANCE

By this time the project team had been disbanded; there was truly nothing they could do during this phase. We did, however, keep everyone in the organization very well informed as to the status of the scheduled activities and availability of deliverables. Finally, after three months, the data had been loaded, reviewed, and signed off. One day I was at a meeting where the discussion revolved around which one of the 35 possibilities was the real system technician name. A manager, who was a peer of my boss, asked the question: "Why don't you ask the data management group?" After all the time and effort invested, this was the first instance of official acceptance; this was the moment when our vision became a part of reality.

Did widespread usage begin the next day? No. Did we begin to have users? Yes. In fact, our first and perhaps most cherished users were the strategic planners. Exactly why this group was the first to recognize the value and thus receive the benefit will probably never be totally clear to me. Nonetheless, I do have some understanding of how it came to be that way. The planners had requests for information from all levels of management (including directors), from many people external to the organization, and naturally from the end user community. None of those individuals had any extensive data processing background, and most of the planners themselves had a business background as opposed to a technical one. Furthermore, the requests were frequently urgent and in order to be addressed thoroughly, multiple systems had to be polled for information. Prior to the advent of data management, they had several equally unattractive options available to them when they needed information. If they were interested in accuracy, the only alternative was the programmers and the code itself. However, that choice had the serious disadvantage that it was highly unlikely they would get the data in a form that would be readily comprehensible to the requestor or even to them. The other alternative, which involved working through the systems analysts, meant that they would have to deal with all the various documents and their inconsistencies. Both options had the additional disadvantage that the planner would have to interact with a substantial number of people.

Once the data management group had accurate information available, there was a third and obviously more palatable option. For example, one of our first requests was initiated by a planner who wanted all the information that we had about system technicians. He did express some concern about timeliness because he needed the report by the next day. We were able to supply him with all the information he required in a few succinct reports, and we had no trouble meeting his deadline. The following day he expressed tremendous gratitude; he told us that everyone else came to the meeting with armloads of documentation. He further stated that without our assistance, he would have had to track down about 25 people in order to obtain the information he needed (see Figures 10–4a and 10–4b).

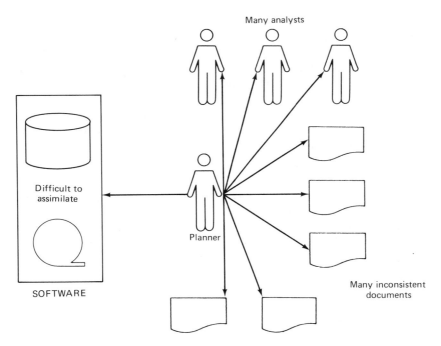

Figure 10–4a Before data management, the alternatives for obtaining information were equally unattractive.

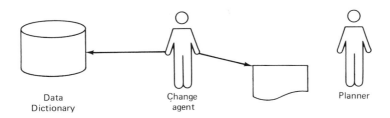

Figure 10–4b After data management, information was readily available that was consistent, concise, comprehensible, and accurate.

There were an increasing number of requests for data as time went by. Ultimately, there did come a moment when our group and our function was unequivocally accepted as the single source of information about our organization's data. This does not mean that every piece of data in every single system was loaded and 100% accurate or that every individual in the organization was wholly committed to our cause. There was an enormous amount of work still ahead of us. But we knew that we had truly and fundamentally changed the way people viewed and utilized data in our environment. We knew beyond a doubt that we had in some profound way improved productivity, and it felt good!

SUMMARY

- The task of actual implementation may seem insurmountable, but you will proceed by dividing the effort into manageable chunks. In fact, many activities of the preliminary phases have set the stage for this.
- If you present your users with too much too soon, they will not be comfortable enough to change. The secret lies in managing change implementation via incremental improvement.
- You can also promote a comfortable situation for people by being flexible and meeting each user on his or her own ground.
- No matter how well you planned, you will encounter numerous unforeseen problems. Dealing with them and the resultant frustration is the essence of the doing phase.
- You may experience a renewal of discouragement and self-doubt, but the secret to success lies in utilization of your abilities to form strategy and persist.

Finishing
the Implementation:
Following Up

This is the phase that in reality never ends; there will always be new users to train, new systems to incorporate, and new management to sell. However, time is finally a friend, and that fact has to do with the phenomena of inertia and momentum. There is a natural tendency to continue almost anything that has been established as an important way for us to be spending our time and effort. It is much easier to persist at a current endeavor than to stop and seriously consider whether or not this is still a valid way to proceed. The act of questioning makes us very uncomfortable because we may discover that whatever we are doing is no longer meaningful. Then we are faced with the possibility that we are wasting our time, which is certainly not an agreeable thought. Consequently, almost never do we initiate this type of reality testing—nor do we tend to react favorably when others initiate it for us. Our tendency is to let things to go on as they are.

This tendency on the part of your users will be perceived by you as the agent of change as inertia during all the phases up to and including implementing change. On the other hand, during the follow-up phase, the tendency will be perceived as momentum because just as it was difficult to get things going, so it is also difficult to stop them once they are in motion. We certainly experienced the phenomenon of inertia during the early phases of our Excelerator implementation. Not only did we assess the situation, analyze the product's projected benefits, and sell them to many people, but the paperwork we completed was quite extensive. We prepared feasibility studies, a business case, a capital appropriations document, and the details of a budget. For each document we prepared, we had to interact with a different group that was providing the coordination function. The combination of document preparation and people interaction consumed considerable time and patience, and these events occurred when we still had other assignments. However, once we had obtained the commitment of management and a core of faithful users, we also experienced the momentum phenomenon. For example, although we were suffering from the effects of cutbacks in our department, our group did not suffer any reductions; in fact, our staff size even increased.

Our management had expended substantial resources in terms of time, people, and money and was not particularly interested in reevaluating that decision at a time when we were making noticeable progress. Our users demonstrated a similar lack of interest in any type of reevaluation when a centralized methods group recommended a different tool as our corporate standard. This recommendation occurred during the follow-up phase, when many of our users were feeling quite comfortable with the tool and beginning to enjoy its benefits.

You should feel very satisfied and proud because you have completed all the other phases of implementing change (see Figure 11–1). Due to the phenomena of inertia and momentum, you can relax a bit, knowing that you will now have substantial opportunities to complete the change process you have set in motion. Indeed, in the months ahead it may seem that change is happening a bit too fast. (In the next chapter, we will point out pitfalls to avoid and ways to combat the momentum.) Having described the existing climate of your organization (and yourself), let us look now at the particular activities you will want to pursue.

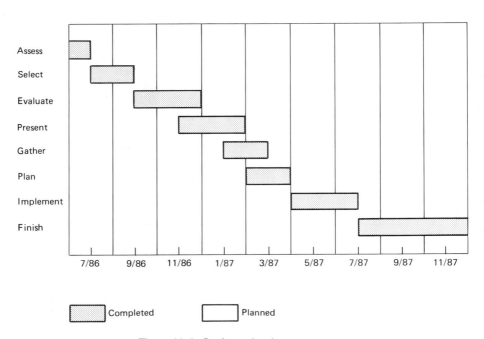

Figure 11–1   Implementing data management.

TRAINING YOUR USERS

One of the primary tasks of this phase will be the training of your user community. In earlier phases, you provided presentations, demonstrations, and generally informed them about the product, its capabilities, and its relevance to them. In other words, you supplied information so that they could understand and appreciate. However, that is not at all the same as providing sufficient detailed information and hands on experience using the product. There are several options that you might pursue to assist you with the provision of this essential service, and it will, as always, vary from tool to tool; however, here are some alternatives we have used successfully:

- Many vendors of the tools and techniques have a training center your users can attend.
- Often, these same vendors will bring the course to you if you have a substantial number of users to train.
- Most packages contain an in-depth demonstration or tutorial that will get many users started.
- Many vendors have developed extensive computer-aided instruction that you can purchase.
- Some vendors will work with the change agents to tailor a course to their specific environment.
- If your company has a training center, you can work with the vendor and your trainers to provide an ongoing course on the tool or technique.
- You can develop your own training course.

You must consider the particular needs of your users, your management, and yourself when you are deciding exactly which method is best for your implementation. The selection will depend on many factors. Here are some:

- The complexity of the product you are implementing
- The quality of the courses that are commercially available
- The amount of money that is available in your organization's budget
- The time your management is willing to allow for training
- The experience level and interest of your user community
- Your own interest and ability in the area of teaching

Although most of these training options are self-explanatory, several will profit from additional discussion. Based on our observations, utilization of the tutorial and computer-aided instruction should be seriously considered. These self-training aids can be so thorough and sophisticated that for data processing veterans and a highly motivated subset of your user community, they will be a sufficient introduction to the product. For example, Project Workbench has an exceptionally easy to use computer-aided instruction for beginners. Moreover, it is so comprehensive that more experienced users employ it as an on-line quick reference guide. For many of our project managers, this was all the training they ever received, yet they were rapidly able to become proficient and sophisticated users.

Bear in mind that budget money can be viewed creatively; the dollars for training may not have to come from the change process budget, but may be drawn from a more general training budget. This determination should be based on the general applicability of the training, because it may not be particularly specific to the productivity improvement. During the follow-up of our data management implementation, people began to seek and obtain training in data analysis and normalization. It was deemed that this training was generally useful to any data processing professional and thus had nothing to do with our budget. Moreover, in that change process there was no urgency on the part of our users or upper management, so time was not an issue.

Sometimes a combination of the various methods can be utilized to meet all the user, change agents, and management requirements. To offer a concrete example of how this was handled for at least one implementation, let us look at how we addressed the training situation when we implemented Excelerator. The first thing we did was to have the vendor give a two-day fundamentals course at our site. We arranged for each group in our organization to have at least one person attend the class. The intent was to supply enough trained individuals to act as seeds; they would then be in a position to train other members of their groups.

The teachers came and the class was taught in an informative and thorough manner; however, afterward we discovered that there were two problems with the way we handled that particular training class. Although the teachers were quite knowledgeable about the tool, they were ignorant about our particular environment. There was no way for them to relate the subject matter to our mode of operation, and many of the students were unable to absorb the material and simultaneously discern ways to apply this knowledge to their jobs. The other problem was related to the diverse abilities and experience levels of our users. The course material covered considerable ground, and what we observed was that the advanced students were bored on the first day, while the second day was beyond the comprehension of the less experienced users.

The technique we used to solve this problem involved one of the other alternatives. We obtained the course materials from the vendor, and with its permission developed our own workshops. This technique allowed us to include numerous real examples illustrating ways to employ Excelerator advantageously in our organization. We also divided the course into two one-day workshops. The fundamentals workshop focused on what a user would need to get started, and the advanced one covered sophisticated topics for the more experienced individual. Dividing the course into one-day workshops had the additional benefit of being less disruptive to the ongoing work of our user community. We found that most users and their managers did not mind sacrificing one day on the job, but they did begin to pause and consider consequences when we asked for two days.

We gained considerable expertise in the area of training while we finished up our implementation of Excelerator. Although we did not offer any diversity initially, by the time we were into the final stages of this effort, the choices available to our users were elaborate. When there was a new release, we had workshops that described the enhancements and how they differed from the earlier version. We had workshops targeted for specific functional groups, such as planners or programmers, since their application of the tool was perhaps not as obvious as that of the systems analysts. There were half-day sessions focused on a particular feature of the product, such as documentation preparation or utilizing the report writer effectively. Completing the tutorial was a prerequisite for the fundamentals course, but we found that many users had trouble setting aside enough time to do so. Therefore, we instituted a tutorial day. We set up half a dozen PCs in a conference room, and a member of our group was constantly in attendance to answer questions. Many users found this a more effective and pleasant way to complete the requirement.

The final chapter in the Excelerator training saga is that since the tool did gain substantial popularity throughout the company, the vendor and some of our corporate groups negotiated a deal. From our perspective, one result of the negotiation was that the course became part of a standard training curriculum. This was a tremendous relief for my group, as we were not particularly interested in becoming teachers.

Before proceeding with other activities of this phase, let's summarize some of the more important aspects of training:

- Training is one of the primary tasks of this phase.
- There are many options available to assist you in providing this service to users.
- The options you select will depend on the product, your organization's budget and time constraints, as well as you, your group, and your users.
- It is likely that you will offer a combination of the alternatives.
- By the end of this phase, you and your group will be quite sophisticated as trainers.

BECOMING A SUPPORT GROUP

If your product is a tool, there will be software support issues that you will have to address at this stage. During our Excelerator implementation, these activities became part of our daily lives. Let's look a little more closely at exactly what that support entailed. We did all the installations on all the PCs for our entire department. Since some of our users were quite inexperienced in technical matters, our installation usually began with a determination of their hardware needs; they might need a mouse or additional memory chips. If they did not have PCs, we facilitated this also; we would, for example, place an initial request with the group responsible for procuring equipment.

We found ourselves supporting not only Excelerator, but also MS-DOS and MS WORD, because it was seldom obvious to our users where one package ended and another began. At particularly frazzled moments it did occur to us to be more rigid about our duties, but we had begun our implementation with a service approach, and we continued it until the day we were reassigned to other jobs.

Since the follow-up phase extended through several releases of the package, we were also responsible for the upgrades. As our user community grew and their use increased, we began to perform some local quality assurance during releases before upgrading our users to new versions of the product. By that time, our staff was substantially larger, so this was an additional service that we were comfortably able to offer.

We also began to serve as trouble shooters. If any user had a problem, we were the first line of support. If we did not find a solution, we were the ones who called the vendor's hotline. This was quite overwhelming at first, but actually turned out to be a reasonably easy service to supply. There was a core of problems and corresponding solutions that occurred and reoccurred, and within two weeks there were very few questions we could not answer immediately. By the end of this phase, the vendor had instituted a formal program that facilitated these interactions. The program assisted groups such as ours which functioned between our users and the vendor's support groups. They provided us with supplementary documentation, bug lists, and priority hotline service.

Let's sum up the activities associated with supporting a productivity tool:

- Determination of associated hardware requirements and facilitation of their acquisition
- Initial installation of the software and all upgrades
- Installation of related software
- First line of support for problems
- Quality assurance when new releases occur

YOU WILL MAKE MISTAKES

After the initial round of the workshops and numerous installations of the tool, we encountered some new and unsuspected sources of resistance. One instance revolved around the fact that many of the projects required additional attributes that were not available on the Excelerator element description form. It was not a question of each project needing different fields; they were all used to the same form of documentation, which included this information. Needless to say, we were worried; these were projects none of us had personal experience with, and somehow we had just overlooked this documentation type.

This story does have a happy ending because the vendor customized our user interface to include the additional fields. Our new users had fields for all their information needs, and the rest of our user community could ignore or use the new fields at their own discretion. This was certainly a shining example of enabling our users to be comfortable as the primary mode of overcoming resistance. There is another point being made here, and that is that anyone can (and will) commit a serious oversight, and this is no cause for a large-scale panic. You must calmly begin the search for a solution; you certainly are creative and resourceful, or you would not be a successful change agent. There is also a footnote to this story. In the midst of the customization process, the vendor replaced its logo with our corporate logo on the welcome screen. This small gesture may have mellowed the hearts of a few skeptics or it may not have; but I enjoyed it immensely.

PREPARING AUXILIARY USER DOCUMENTATION

Another goal that we recommend you accomplish during the early stages of the follow-up phase is to prepare a user guide. This document is not meant to replace any guide prepared by the vendor, which is meant to be employed when users are becoming acquainted with the tool or technique. Your user guide will be a supplementary document for survival in your specific and unique environment. A typical table of contents might be as follows:

1. Introduction
2. How to Get Started
3. Who to Contact
4. Standards and Naming Conventions
5. Change Control
6. Version Control
7. Roles and Responsibilities

This document should be quite easy to prepare. After all, the basis for virtually all the information it will contain has already been developed by you, your group, your interproject team, and your users. Another point worth mentioning is that this should be a living document because you are committed to never developing standards, naming conventions, etc., until they are actually needed.

FORMING A USER GROUP

Another pursuit you should seriously consider is the possibility of forming a user group at this time. User groups can be a powerful means for keeping the change process progressing in a vital manner. Below is a list of a few of the benefits to be gained from the formation, operation, and continuance of such a group:

- The group provides an effective means for obtaining information.
- It offers a vehicle to communicate your opinions, beliefs, and experiences to a large audience.

- There will be opportunities for beginners to learn from the experts.
- A user organization can establish a channel for sharing associated products, such as user-supplied software.
- The sharing that takes place can include unresolved problems users encounter.
- The group can present a strong, united, collective voice to the vendor.

Certainly there will always remain areas about which even the most experienced user would like more information. The advanced user will hear about unique and interesting applications of the tool and perhaps receive information about training that will be offered locally in the near future. The beginners (who may be experiencing severe problems or don't even know how to get started) will be heartened by the success stories of others. You can also take advantage of the chance to extend your informal network; there is, after all, no reason to limit it to your company.

One user group to which I belonged established a user software library. Users were encouraged to donate routines they had developed to enhance the capabilities of the tool itself. These routines were made available to other users free of charge. We even sponsored a contest to boost the rate of software submission. I'm not sure how well we succeeded in our encouragement, but it was fun!

The last items on the list are probably the most important of all. It is critical that the user group arena be utilized to share not only success stories, but also the problems or even failures users encounter. It may well be that another user has had a similar disastrous experience. Moreover, she may have figured out a way to resolve the problem, which she can then share with the group. If there is no resolution, the group can present a substantial and loud protest to the vendor. This collective voice to the vendor leads directly into the final item on the list. It is certainly true that the group can be a powerful and effective lobby to achieve common goals in connection with the vendor. However, this may seem quite negative, considering that most of our experiences have indicated that vendors do actually welcome opportunities to have users' needs clearly communicated.

Now that we have convinced you there are some definite advantages to be gained by the formation of such a group, let's turn our attention to how you might accomplish this task. Since I was once involved in the formation of a local user group, the details of its history will be immediately shared. After conceiving the idea, the first thing I did was mention it to my current boss. This man was a very bright and enthusiastic individual, and consequently was quite taken with the idea. Moreover even though I was extremely busy at this time, he encouraged me to reserve some of my energy to pursue this possibility.

With his solid support behind me, I approached the vendor's eastern region sales manager, Paul, with my idea. I wanted to determine if he was interested; and if he was, how much support he would give to the effort. He was an experienced data processing individual with exceptionally astute and progressive views. He immediately and fully grasped the benefits for us all. Paul and I drafted a letter stating the possibility of forming a local user group and soliciting interest. He had his clerical support staff prepare the letter and mail it to all current and potential users in the NY/NJ metropolitan area. We decided that we would both sign the letter to indicate that the group would be a joint endeavor of the vendor and user community. The response was overwhelming; apparently many people were able to perceive the usefulness of such a group.

We set the date for the first meeting, reserved a conference room, and began to plan the agenda. We decided to have several users share their experiences, and we elected to have a few people from the vendor company speak on topics such as features planned in the next release. Paul's staff prepared and mailed the invitations while I, who was to give one of the user presentations, began to prepare for the event. The user group got off to a very nice start, and to the best of my knowledge is still active today. The group meets about three times a year, the users take turns providing the room, and the vendor's staff still prepares and mails the meeting notices.

Here is a list of steps we recommend you follow to form a user group:

- Obtain management sanction for your endeavor because of the initial expenditure of effort on your part.
- Solicit the cooperation and support of your local vendor representative.
- Determine if there is sufficient interest on the part of the local user community.
- Arrange the first meeting with speakers representing both the users and the vendor.
- Maintain group continuity by holding meetings several times a year.
- Share the responsibility by rotating the hosting of meetings among the users, and arranging for continuance of support from the vendor.

YOUR ROLE AS A CONSULTANT

Thus far we have described several major activities that you will perform during the follow-up. There is an additional one that will be a critical success factor. Several months into this phase, you will begin to assume the role of consultant; in that capacity, you will present multiple services. You will consult to individuals, groups, and all levels of management. The most conspicuous aspect of this role is that you will be a paradigm of flexibility. For example, we provided individualized consulting to users who had taken the workshop, were ready to apply the knowledge, but were still unsure. One of us would spend several days with him, while he began the definition of enhancements to the next system release. Following that initial period, he might call us about once an hour for a week. Then the calls would become farther and farther apart. Finally, several months later, we would hear that he was consulting for another project!

We might approach a group and offer to help them use the product to perform their present assignment. We promised that we would work with them so they could accomplish it at least as fast as they always did. If our claims were even half true, they would complete the task in substantially less time. Our hope was that the next time they wanted to use the tool, they would probably not need our help. Did every group we approach accept our offer? Of course not. But there were certainly enough interested users to keep us busy. That was the most gratifying aspect of the follow-up phase; there are so many ways to continue the implementation. If you approached one group of users and they were disinterested or too busy, you could approach another group who was already amenable. Once the interested group began exhibiting some improvement, the first group you approached may well perceive some benefit, and find some time after all to become involved.

RESIDUAL RESISTANCE

I would be untruthful if I did not admit that there were some individuals we just could not convert. They obstinately refused to even consider the possibilities, and continued to find problem after problem with the product. They did not understand what was wrong with the way they were currently doing their job. They were much too busy to spare even an hour to allow us to provide information. They thought the tool was far too expensive. (Since this comment was made a year after purchase, it was particularly irrelevant.) There was even one fellow who wanted to rewrite the user interface not because it was inadequate, but because he could do it. Moreover, most of these people were intelligent and aggressive, and many had considerable personal power in their groups.

If it was at all possible, we ignored the unconverted. After all, we had plenty of people who were interested and we were still few in number. When our director inquired about how we were handling the users who still exhibited considerable resistance, I told her not to worry about them. They would have to join us eventually, because ultimately there would be no other choice left. Some of these people we outlasted; they transferred or changed companies. In the case of a very few, their managers exerted considerable pressure and they did finally participate. There is no solution to this problem; you will just have to face some failures. It does not mean that your effort is not still a smashing success, but only that change agents are human beings not magicians.

THE STRATEGY MEETING

One of the most successful means that we utilized in our consultant role was the strategy meeting. We would invite a project team to meet briefly with us for the following purposes:

- To ensure that they were fully aware of the value of the tool

- To allow them the opportunity to review all the information already available that could be used via the tool
- To allow us the opportunity to examine all the documents they were currently utilizing to help develop their system
- To jointly set a strategic direction for them to gradually incorporate the tool without disruption

At a typical meeting, they might discover that all the screens for their user guide had already been entered into Excelerator. This fact would certainly cause them to consider seriously the appropriateness of using the tool at this time. Usually they would bring every document they used as a development aid to the meeting, and we would go through every one page by page. There would be an exchange of ideas about the feasibility of using the tool for each portion of each document at this time. We would almost always recommend they use the tool for the record layouts, the screens, and the reports. Furthermore, we would point out how the data flow diagrams could be used to depict their functional requirements. But if they were not thoroughly familiar with the technique, we would also recommend they delay that use of the tool until their next release (and accompanying definition phase).

We were this cautious because we had not forgotten the principle of ensuring a series of small successes. There was also an element of the comfort factor at work. It was certainly a goal that each use of the tool should be accompanied by a corresponding increase in user confidence. We did not even hint that anyone should change the format of their documentation; every project still retained its individualized approach to system development. But we did offer some consistency in the piece parts that comprised each document (see Figure 11–2).

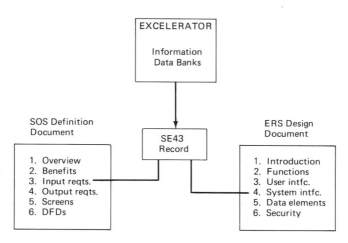

Figure 11–2 Regulation bricks ensure consistency of information content but allow documentation to be individualized.

The analogy of building houses is a good one. If one group preferred colonial style, they would still be building a colonial; if another group liked California ranches, they would still be building a ranch. What was new in the process was that everyone would now be building the foundation with regulation bricks that were the same size, color, and weight. The main aspect of this situation that facilitated the steady progress of the change process was that the documentation looked almost exactly as it always had to the systems analysts, the programmers, and the users. There was no abrupt and disruptive change; it was as always before in the process: unfaltering, smooth, and gradual.

During the implementation phase, we indicated that at the beginning of the follow-up phase you would have a small core of dedicated users. Furthermore, there would be a widespread belief throughout the organization that your productivity improvement was available and thus a part of the current environment. But we warned you not to deceive yourself into believing more has been accomplished than actually has. For example, the majority of the people will smile approval at you and your group, but proceed as they always have. We have also indicated that a certain level of disinterest is really not a problem, because you and your group are still small in number and there will be enough interested users to keep you very busy.

During the first stages of the follow-up phase, we have described many techniques you can employ to increase your user base. This should be a pleasurable part of the process; you will not be pressed to deliver specifics in a short time. You will have the luxury of selecting the groups you will work with. The fruits of your labor should begin to be apparent. In general, you will be solidifying your success. You earned it and you should enjoy it, because there are still some significant hazards ahead.

SUMMARY

- This is the phase that never ends because there will always be new users to train and new managers to sell; however, due to the momentum of the change effort, there will be plenty of time to accomplish any task that needs to be done.

- One of the primary tasks of this phase will be teaching, and there will be a number of alternatives available.

- If your product is a tool, you will find yourself in the position of supporting the software itself as well as associated software and hardware.

- Consider the possibility of developing a user guide which will document aspects of the change that are particular to your specific environment.

- The formation of a local user group is an effective means to keep your change process vital. It will afford an arena for information sharing and collective communication with the vendor.

- Considerable time and effort will be expended during this phase in your role as a consultant; one of the most powerful techniques you will utilize will be the strategy meeting.

12

Finishing the Implementation: Averting Disasters

Although the most difficult tasks of the change process are behind you, there exist, as a natural consequence of success, some very powerful obstacles that you must overcome. In the last chapter we described the phenomena of inertia and momentum, and we indicated that as the change process progressed, so would the momentum progress. Moreover, we suggested the real possibility that while momentum is favorable, it can also gain too much force. Remember the pitfall of too much too soon; that is something you must guard against throughout the entire implementation of the productivity improvement.

As the product gains in popularity, there will be more and more people who are willing to experiment with it. Consequently, there will be an enormous temptation to spread yourself too thin. Over the course of the last year, you have adopted an orientation of service and cooperation, so it will be very difficult for you consciously to limit your function. However, you must do so. The problems that result from too much too soon in the apocryphal tale of Chapter 10 apply in this situation also. If you attempt to supply each individual or group with the same level of commitment you previously offered, the result will be a serious decline in quality. Since you are dealing with improvement and productivity, you cannot afford to have the quality of the effort decrease. Therefore, what you must do is continue to search selectively for small successes. Bear in mind that there is no way you can improve everyone's work life at once; help the most capable, and then they may help some of the others. On the other hand, there are alternatives available so that you do not ignore and alienate potential users. You can always provide information: give them product literature, a copy of your user guide, and the names of the super users on other projects. This level of service may be just right for their current level of need, and it establishes a basis for future positive interaction.

THE REORGANIZATION: A SLICE OF REALITY

We have made you aware of the dangers related to voluntarily assuming more responsibility than you are able to handle. Now we will offer advice about how to deal with a situation when you are involuntarily made responsible for more than you can manage. The most common cause that precipitates this situation is the reorganization. In order to paint a striking example of what might occur, we will share the events that occurred during the follow-up phase of the data management implementation.

When we last heard about this particular productivity improvement, the data management group had been accepted as the official source of information. During the initial stages of the follow-up phase, Sally and I performed many of the tasks described in the previous chapter: We drafted a user guide, provided consulting services and performed the ongoing activities of data administration. Our user base steadily increased, support and even enthusiasm were often expressed, and our upper management was very pleased. In fact, they were so pleased that they decided to reorganize the group. Thus three months into the follow-up phase found us reorganized into the planning division so that we could perform data management not only for our department, but for the entire section. This meant that the scope of our responsibility had tripled, and the two levels of management between myself and the director were changed. Moreover, four very inexperienced people were transferred into the group, and Sally went on maternity leave.

Initially I was gratified by this acknowledgment of our success and the increased responsibility; and I even mentally congratulated us for our tactical planning abilities. We had foreseen this reorganization during the planning phase, and had ensured that our procedures, standards, etc., accommodated the other groups in our section (see Chapter 8). Therefore we would not have to cause any disruption in the manner in which we interacted with our users. But as I was soon to discover, there were other issues to consider at this stage. For example, we now had the problem of providing service for three times as many users, while simultaneously gathering, analyzing, and loading a substantial amount of new data. Furthermore, that was only one issue. The whole change effort was in jeopardy, and I spent many sleepless nights casting about for a method to avert disaster. Actually, in retrospect, I am convinced that this is the first step in dealing with a crisis of this magnitude; you must face the fact that you are in a perilous situation. Having made that assessment, you are at least not wasting energy denying reality and are thus free to reason your way out of the problem.

While you are figuring out your course of action, you must not share your anxiety with anyone. It will not increase your new management's or your new group's confidence in your abilities if you are visibly upset and insecure. We are not suggesting that you lie; if your new boss inquires about potential problems with the new group structure and placement in the organization, you should definitely mention your concerns. But you must do so calmly and with the implicit assurance that you will deal with them. There are several reasons to point out the problems if asked to do so, the most obvious one being that if you gave the impression that everything was perfect and then the change effort came to a grinding halt, you would not be in an enviable position. More important, since you are going to save the situation, you do want your new manager to have registered the problems so that he will mentally give you credit for the solutions. It really comes down to the fact that unnoticed heroics will not assist the implementation of the productivity improvement or your career.

In addition to not wandering around airing your concerns when they have not been solicited, you must also not lose your nerve about commitments. It is imperative that you continue to publicly share your goals and be willing to be held accountable. You should, however, be realistic; and that means that you factor into the equation that you do now have a staff and that they are inexperienced. Moreover, we do not mean to imply that you will in all areas be doing less, because there will be some services you will be able to provide even more effectively. For example, we were getting numerous requests for reports, and within days our new staff was able to meet this need more rapidly. Thus, there are some benefits to be gained from your new staff that are realizable quite quickly.

Although the example we have described may not be exactly mirrored in your case, there may well be many similarities. Therefore, let's list the issues that may be brought about by a reorganization:

- The very success of your effort may be the force that precipitates the reorganization.
- The result may be that your entire management chain has been changed.
- You may also suddenly discover yourself with a substantial and inexperienced staff.
- No matter how well you have planned, you will not be truly prepared for the new responsibilities.
- The first step toward resolving some of your problems is to face the severity of the situation.
- You must not share your anxiety with either your management or your new staff.
- If information is solicited, you should point out the obvious problems in this situation.
- You are not permitted to stop making commitments or to become less cooperative during adverse times.
- Immediately put your new staff to work; you will be pleasantly surprised by what they can absorb and accomplish right away.

DEALING WITH YOUR NEW STAFF

The last item on the list is directly related to our next topic of discussion, dealing with your new staff. Even though you may be discouraged, it is important to visualize clearly that they will soon be experienced and quite competent. Moreover, in spite of the numerous demands on you at this time, you must expend substantial energy in supervising and training the group. You cannot ever afford to forget that before you even had the role of change agent, you were a manager and hence a developer of people. There may be no greater sin that a supervisor can commit than to allow people to be bored; hence your primary goal in this role is to ensure that each of your staff members has a meaningful job. A meaningful job can be characterized as one that is challenging to the individual and requires full attention all day long. The art of accomplishing this feat easily is one of the secrets of being a successful manager. In fact, if you were not motivated in this direction by an obligation to your people, there is a practical and selfish reason for doing so. Training people to be effective change agents is really your only hope for saving the situation; so somehow you must make it a priority to achieve this objective fast.

But how to achieve this objective under your present circumstances may not be at all clear. One way to begin might be by listing all the responsibilities and objectives of your group. Then try to cluster tasks that might comprise a well-rounded full-time job. This document does not have to be elaborate, nor should it require a lot of time and energy. You simply cannot waste effort on formality. A draft document with listed items is more than adequate. For example, after some reflection, it may occur to you that you need a technical support person to perform the following activities:

- Installation of PC software packages and associated hardware support
- System administration for the UNIX/3B minicomputer
- Selection of local area network hardware and software to link the mini and the PCs
- Development of conversion software to mechanically update the data dictionary used by the UNIX DBMS
- Trouble shooting and technical consultation for problems

You may also determine that you need a systems analyst to perform these activities:

- Gather the documentation from the new user groups
- Analyze the data requirements based on these documents
- Compare and analyze the new data and the data already in the dictionary to avoid creating redundant elements
- Perform logical database design and normalization

Next you want to assess each individual in terms of experience, ability, personality type, and interest; and then match each person with a particular job. This isn't too difficult; (remember how you decided who was going to perform the evaluation in Chapter 3). But don't assume too much; make sure you talk to each person. Finally, use common sense; give the technical support job to the woman who can install software packages on the most exotic hardware—the one who carries a screwdriver and spare memory chips around with her at all times.

Now that you have the various jobs defined and individuals targeted for each one of them; you will need to evolve a plan to enable each of them to become fully functional. For each individual, reflect on exactly which tasks their jobs will entail and analyze the skills they will have to acquire. You also need to determine the areas in which you most urgently require help. Attempt to assess how difficult it will be for each person to learn each skill. You will have to weigh your need, the person's experience, and balance this against the time constraints and difficulties of obtaining training. Finally, you can come up with a prioritized list that details the order in which they will be trained for each task. Figures 12–1a through 12–1d illustrate the steps in this process. For example, in the case of the technical support job outlined above, it should be reasonably easy to teach your guru the installation and upgrade procedures. This might not be the area where you most need assistance, but it will remove one burden. On the other hand, you want to avoid personally teaching skills that are complex. In the systems analyst job described above, we recommend sending the individual for formal training to learn logical database design and normalization techniques. Teaching those skills (particularly at this time) would be a serious drain on the already overworked resources of the change agent.

We have discussed in detail the assignment of responsibilities to your new staff members. We have also suggested several ways for you to actualize these assignments. So before we proceed with advice on interacting with your new management, let's summarize:

Figure 12–1a   Cluster all the tasks of your group into discrete jobs.

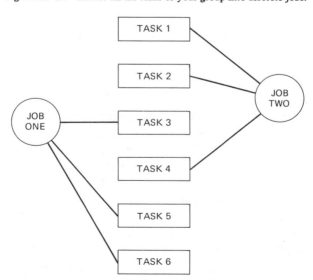

Person A   Person B

Figure 12–1b Assess each group member.

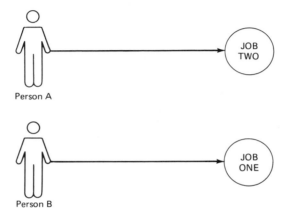

Figure 12–1c Target each group member for a specific job.

1. Prioritize tasks.
2. Identify skills they must acquire.
3. Assess difficulty of acquisition.
4. Develop training plan.

Figure 12–1d Enable each group member to perform job fully.

- In your enthusiasm as a change agent, never forget your role as a supervisor.
- This role includes the development of your people, especially as it relates to defining a meaningful job for each of them.
- Job descriptions can be developed by listing and then clustering all the responsibilities and objectives of your group.
- Taking into account each individual's experience and interest, assign each person to a job.
- Develop a plan to enable each group member to become fully functional.
- Factor into the equation your own needs and resources at the time.
- Do not expend precious time and energy preparing formal documents, because lists of items are more than adequate.

DEALING WITH YOUR NEW MANAGEMENT

Now we need to concentrate on dealing with your new management. Because you are so far along in the change process, abandonment of the productivity improvement is not a serious threat. However, during the follow-up phase of the data management implementation we did find that with each new manager, there was a shift in priorities. Shifting priorities can present significant problems.

At one point the data management group was working for a visionary manager, and therefore we were in the midst of redoing the data architecture for our section (this scenario will be discussed in detail in Chapter 14). Following a surprise reorganization, we found ourselves working for a very practical management team. They were not at all interested in a course of action that would require several years and consist of a gradual migration to subject databases. Their highest priority was to have each programmer change the name of every data element to a common name in every program so that we would have consistency. In fact, my manager's manager stated unequivocally that he would not believe he had gained anything through data management until it was reflected in the code!

This scenario may sound vaguely familiar. During our implementation of Excelerator, we described a similar suggestion which was proposed by a planner on the project team. We discussed our rejection of this idea and our reasons (see Chapter 9). In the data management case, we had bypassed this option during the previous regime because it just did not seem worth the effort. If we were to modify all the code in all our systems' software, then we believed fervently that the result must be a state-of-the-art architecture, which surely would include subject databases. Although at this stage we had not progressed much further than assessing the need, we were wholly committed to this course of action.

What must (and did) happen in these cases is that you resume the role of salesperson and you sell the new management, just as you sold the original management. The sales pitch, however, is different for several reasons. You should by this stage of the implementation have numerous, substantial, and tangible benefits to display, so there should be immediate acceptance of the credibility of your effort. Conversely, you do not as yet have influence and personal power with your new boss. In the original situation, you had to sell the product; in the present situation, you have to sell yourself. (Actually, to ensure your political safety, you need to do this whether or not you are an agent of change.)

There is no script for this one, because you will be endeavoring to steadily improve the dynamic interaction between yourself and another person (your new boss). The interaction will, of course, vary from individual to individual, but there are some techniques (such as empathy) which you have utilized throughout the change process that should be extremely helpful. For example, you will be tempted to immediately enlighten your new boss about your mission, its history, and its purpose; however, he may be suffering from an overdose of information. Don't add to his load by detailing the entire implementation in one session; practice effective listening. Then you can take your cue from him, be flexible, and apply the technique of meeting him on his own ground. If he is indeed a detail person, give him copies of all your documents. He can read them at his leisure and call you when he has questions. If he is suffering from overload, treat him the same way you treat your very busy upper management. But don't assume, pay attention, get the lay of the land, and employ the skills you have developed along the way. All this will quickly build up a level of trust and confidence that will result in your possessing enough influence to reshift the priorities.

Let's pause and recap what the reorganization may mean to you in terms of your management:

- Changes in your management will surely result in a shift of priorities.
- This shift may result in a direction that is both dramatically different and unacceptable to the fundamental philosophy of your effort.
- You must resume the role of salesperson to achieve a resumption of the original priorities.
- This time the purpose of your sales pitch is to sell yourself, not the product.
- You will utilize skills that you have developed throughout the change process to create the proper environment between yourself and your new boss.

MODULARITY AND CONTINUITY OF APPROACH

Even after I began to train my new staff and unload some of the work into their increasingly competent hands and I had begun to win the trust and confidence of my new boss, I remained in a serious situation. It was certainly to my credit that I had hastily developed a plan and once again laid the groundwork for the proper environment, but there were still some difficulties that related to the doing. My problem was directly related to the integrity of the new data dictionary. The one aspect of this change that made it so attractive was that finally there was a user-friendly and reliable source of information. My quandary involved the thought of sacrificing this security and integrity by allowing an inexperienced staff to update the dictionary. Of course, if I did not allow them to update the dictionary, not only would new projects not get included, but they would not be able to learn their jobs.

My solution to this paradox was modularity. I partitioned the data so that what had already been loaded was in one portion of the dictionary. I then established a new partition for the data associated with the new departments we were now also responsible for. There was a natural division of the data, since one set of systems was for operations support and another was for management information. Since there was some overlap of data elements, I created a concept of ownership; only one partition owned each data element, and that was the only place it could be updated. Then I personally managed the original data that already had a high degree of integrity and was in use. I put my new staff to work on the other partition so the new data could be loaded, analyzed, and verified. This meant that I worked weekends for about a month, but I was determined that there would always be at least a portion of the data that would be valid and thus truly useful (see Figure 12–2).

This concept of modularity can be extended to any productivity tool or technique. The basic idea is similar to manageable chunks; i.e. you can modularize the change that has already taken place by dividing it back into the chunks that were managed or already implemented. Once you mentally reverse the process, you can ensure that the productivity improvement that has already been accomplished remains useful. Remember the concept of intermediate goals; this modularity is a continuation of that objective. The goal becomes not only to deliver, but always to maintain something that is beneficial to the user.

The other technique that can be very important, especially during periods of adversity is what we call "continuity of approach." This is really nothing more than continuing your commitment to a service orientation. Even though you are pressed by many problems, your attitude must not become less cooperative and helpful. Furthermore, you will have to instill this attitude in your new staff. If they do not always have solutions for the users, at least they will be friendly, helpful, and make every attempt to supply all the needed information. Since your staff is steadily increasing their knowledge base, they will soon be able to solve more and more problems. Then, because they have both the knowledge and the proper attitude, the user community will want to interact with your group as well as with you.

The techniques we have just described are very important. You might want to review their salient features, as stated below:

- Modularity provides a way to maintain what is already useful and beneficial to your users.
- Continuity of approach applies not only to yourself, but extends to your new staff.

Figure 12–2   Modularity was concretely employed by partitioning the data dictionary.

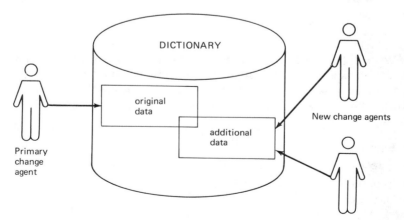

- Both techniques enable you to offer products and services that are worthwhile even under adverse circumstances.

REEVALUATE THE PLAN

Following a reorganization, you may have to face an adversity that is related to peripheral people resources in your previous and current organizations. In our case study, we experienced direct impact to one of our work items when we were moved to the planning division. We had on our schedule activities to implement a local area network so that our users could have on-line access to the data dictionary. When we developed that schedule, we were part of the technical support district and thus had considerable expertise available to complete the activities. After we were reorganized, there was no one in our new division with the technical background required to implement the local area network. Considering that we had survived for a year without the LAN, and considering all the other situations I had to address at that time, I relegated this one to the bottom of my list.

The story about our LAN work item should convey that whenever there is a major organizational change, it behooves the people who are implementing productivity improvements to reevaluate all scheduled activities. Actually not blindly adhering to the schedule but rather constantly reassessing the situation is a skill acquired in the doing phase. Thus the message you should absorb at this point is that you need to continue exercising that technique for the rest of the change effort. At any stage it may well be the case that some voluntary shifting of priorities will not only alleviate some stress, but may actually improve the rate of implementation. In our case we had originally planned to load all the data into dictionary in the following order:

- Interfaces
- Databases
- Screens
- Reports

We had scheduled the databases second because as part of technical support, we were organizationally and geographically close to the programmers. After the reorganization we were organizationally and geographically close to our end users, and thus it made sense to load the user view into the dictionary next. Our amended schedule was as follows:

- Interfaces
- Screens
- Reports
- Databases

Since the screens and reports were much better documented (via user guides), the percentage of data loaded was increased more rapidly.

In Chapter 6, we introduced our experience with data management, and at that time addressed the same issues when we described brainstorming activities. The summary there contained three items that apply at this time also:

- Select an alternative with a very high probability of success.
- Consider very carefully your resources and the potential effect they could have (or their lack could have) on any given approach.
- Make sure you use your resource analysis to increase the chances of success.

Notice how the themes of the earlier phases are reiterated again and again, particularly when you are finishing the implementation. This is no accident; the issues do not change, but you are still dealing with people and all the unpredictability this represents. Thus you will continually encounter unplanned obstacles, which you can now begin to view as challenges. After all, at this juncture you certainly possess considerable expertise in all the skills required to be a successful change agent.

ATTEMPTED POLITICAL TAKEOVERS

Although the reorganization is the most severe hazard that can occur, it is by no means the only one. Another major area of conflict is also related to the success of the implementation thus far. Up till now, except for some minor skirmishes during the interproject team days, no one has considered you a competitive threat. However, now that the productivity improvement has become popular and is enjoying a fair amount of attention, you must prepare to defend your stronghold. In our case, what happened at this stage was that a significant number of people suddenly became data analysts and many projects were unexpectedly (and amateurishly) normalizing their data.

There are a number of ways to combat this situation; and for some of them you have already laid the groundwork—the "roles and responsibilities" document you and the interproject team developed. The significance of this document at this particular juncture is that it clearly defines your turf. Moreover, the fact that it was prepared by the team strengthens your position; it is likely that individuals from the same group as your opponents helped develop the document and thus shape your collective destiny. That it did not come solely from your group but was a product of the organization goes a long way toward discrediting your opponents. Their claim for the reasonableness of their performing your group's job functions was surrendered long ago in the planning stage. If they persist, it is even possible that they will antagonize some of their co-workers who were and are part of the change process.

The only action you must take is to ensure that the document is recirculated at this time. You also want to make sure that your management is aware of its existence, its history, and its current relevance, because they may have some political issues to resolve with their peers. In fact, this may be an optimal time for you to begin providing your boss with some additional details about the implementation. You both have had some time to adjust, and by now the foundation of the relationship has been paved with mutual trust and confidence.

Last, try to devise ways for you and your group to be highly visible when these political issues arise. Heightened visibility will reaffirm your position as well as further establish the position of all levels of your new management. As we mentioned previously, during times of stress it is not likely that the implementation will come to a halt, but conflict drains the resources of everyone associated with the change. It is your objective to reduce the stress, so anything you can do to present the change effort in a positive light will help. You might, for example, arrange a presentation of the current status of available information and its usefulness.

TAKING A STRONGER STAND

As you gain political strength, there may be a tendency on your part or some pressure on you by your management to take a slightly stronger stand. This small adjustment of orientation may be very appropriate; it could well be the exact moment to lean a little on the project that was always so evasive. Possibly the manager has a history of expressing interest, but you can never get a commitment for an hour of her time. Send her a memo which states the same objectives you would have for any strategy meeting—information exchange and mutual direction setting (see Chapter 11 for details on the strategy meeting). In addition, provide at least five specific days and times that you are available within the next two weeks. Carbon copy your boss for the twin purposes of enabling him to pursue this if he so desires, and allowing the other manager to know your offer is public knowledge. All this will make it very difficult for her to continue ignoring you.

You may recall that in Chapter 8, we described a type of power struggle that is of a passive nature. The difficult individual exhibits extreme nonconformity, such as agreeing with all team members but then pursuing a direction in opposition to the team's efforts. We pointed out that this behavior is not only very resistant to positive overtures from the team leader, but severely demoralizes the team. Our experience indicates that the situation is not hopeful, and we advised removing this individual from the team if at all possible. If this was not an option, we promised final resolution of this problem in this chapter. Well, the moment has arrived: If she is still in your organization and still persisting in her maddening ways, your opportunity to address the situation is at hand. Very simply, you now have so much power that even the most stubborn of souls will no longer be able or willing to fight you.

We had a firsthand experience with a case such as this one when we implemented Excelerator. One project team member followed this pattern in every one of its annoying details. Since there was no possibility of her removal from the team, we existed with some considerable frustration. While the team was establishing standards and naming conventions, she was assigned (as project leader) to what was deemed to be the most important development project in our organization. She did not follow even one of the rules we had evolved, and thus the name of every single entity (elements, records, processes, etc.) in her system was different from those in any other system. This disparity did not lend itself to identifying redundancy and possible common routines. We handled the situation by manually renaming every entity when her system went into production. Due to the fact that I was not able to impress her with the seriousness of the inconvenience to my group, I approached her boss. I explained the situation to her manager and said we would never convert everything manually again. By that time I had attained enough power (both positional and personal) to enforce this claim. Our rugged individualist was in the end forced to a humdrum life of conformity.

As you can see, many different perilous situations may arise while you are finishing your implementation; we have mentioned only a few possibilities. However, the suggestions we offered should be generally applicable to help you resolve most of the crises. Here is a summary of the issues we have discussed:

- The reorganization is not the only adversity you will encounter once your change effort is widely perceived as successful.
- You may now be viewed as a competitive threat, and hence must be prepared to defend your turf.
- This will be made easier for you because of the "roles and responsibilities" document the project team developed during the planning phase.
- You now have enough political strength to exert pressure in some areas where you have been tolerating considerable frustration.

One final thought about your political interactions; do not lose sight of your goal to create the proper environment in which change can take place. It may be appropriate to utilize some of the political strength you now clearly possess, but do so judiciously and gently. We have stressed the importance of instilling in your users both trust and confidence in you, your group, and the change effort itself. Maintaining the proper environment is also critical for continued success. You really do not want to undo your effort with a senseless display of power. Moreover, you must also feel confidence and trust in your users; confidence in their willingness and ability to participate in the change process, and trust that they will be sincere and fair. We have found that it is better to start from a position of confidence and trust until it is clear that this is misplaced. If you do so, more times than not, it will be justified. If you do not do so, then it will not be possible to expect others to have confidence and trust in you, and there is no hope for ever achieving that proper environment.

SUMMARY

- Your success in implementing the productivity improvement will precipitate some very powerful obstacles that you must overcome.
- You must guard against voluntarily assuming more than you can handle, as well as dealing with involuntarily being made responsible for too much via a reorganization.
- Following a reorganization, you will have to re-create the proper environment; this includes selling your new management, and supervising and training your new group.
- Properly supervising and training your group is a basic component of your job as a manager. Moreover, it is your only hope for salvation, so make it a priority.
- To maintain the level of success you have already achieved, you will use the techniques of modularity and continuity of approach.
- You will now have substantial political power and it will be appropriate to utilize some of it, but do so judiciously and gently.

13

Finishing the Implementation: Measuring the Benefit

We would be less than honest if we did not admit that currently it is not truly possible to measure productivity gains in a manner that can withstand scientific scrutiny. There are certainly many explanations for such a claim, and the most compelling factor has to do with the essence of productivity itself. Let us try to capture the dilemma by examining a specific productivity improvement such as our implementation of Excelerator for analyst support.

PROBLEMS ASSOCIATED WITH MEASURING

Before we began this implementation, morale was poor and the situation was less than optimal in our organization. We were nevertheless enhancing our systems and developing new ones. Were these systems delivered on time and basically error-free? Seldom. Were they terribly late and totally disappointing to the users? No. But there was a notable lack of enthusiasm, energy, and teamwork, as well as over-all control and quality. As we proceeded in our self-assigned roles as missionaries, did we begin to deliver our systems on time more frequently, or did they have fewer errors? Not always. Was the overall quality of work life better near the end of the follow-up phase? Definitely. Was any improvement directly attributable to Excelerator? The answer is that it remains unclear. Was the improvement related at all? Almost certainly. But what remains ambiguous is the extent and exact amount.

In fact, the parameters we would attempt to measure are indisputably un-defined. If our releases began to be delivered ahead of schedule, it could be that they contained less functionality than previous releases. Possibly serendipity was involved, and although functionality (from a user perspective) was greatly increased, the enhancements were trivial because of the original system design or architecture. Perhaps the last release required half the number of people to develop it and yet was still delivered on schedule. Then the doubters would question their experience level; did all the junior people leave the project? Maybe those who remained just got better at performing their jobs.

In the case of our systems analysts, even the fact that their morale was conspicuously improved was suspect. Prior to the advent of Excelerator, we were in the midst of budget cuts and the accompanying force reductions. Conversely, by the end of our implementation, the situation was one of growth, with possibilities of promotions and substantial raises. We would be hard pressed to demonstrate that improving productivity was the sole or even major contributing factor to increased user happiness.

Having begun with such an unequivocal statement, and then proceeding to prove that measuring may well be infeasible, you may be wondering how long this chapter will be. But the fact is that you must measure something, and you must ensure that whatever you do choose to measure is as meaningful as possible. After all, you launched this productivity effort with a business case that surely contained projected benefits. You are now close enough to the end of the implementation to face the reality of whether or not you have truly improved the environment. If you are not curious, you can be certain your upper management will be very interested. Don't forget these are the people who demand to see numbers and quantifiable benefits. You were well aware of that sentiment in the beginning, and it still exists at the end.

Before we proceed with our suggestions for handling this quandary, let's summarize some of the difficulties inherent in measuring productivity gains:

- At the present time there are no scientific and widely accepted methods of measuring improvements in productivity.
- The problem resides in the difficulty of isolating exactly which parameters are being measured.
- There is also considerable subjectivity associated with any parameter that is selected.
- Nevertheless, it is imperative that you measure something, because even if you are not interested, your management will be.

Now that we have presented this seemingly insolvable dilemma, we do, of course, have some very practical ways to approach a solution. We have evolved techniques to prove the "added value" of data management that may not have even approached measuring productivity. They did, however, fulfill an obligation that we had to develop and measure our goals and objectives. Furthermore, when we implemented Excelerator, we actually measured the productivity improvement four different ways during the final stages of this phase. While bearing in mind that none of these methods have any widespread scientific acceptance, they did instill our management with a certain level of satisfaction in the economic justification of the change effort.

STATUS REPORTS

In the data management case, one method we employed was to publish a bimonthly status report of the percentage complete of the data load. Moreover, each different type of data (elements, records, screens, etc.) was displayed on a system per system basis. Figure 13–1 contains a sample of this type of report. You will notice some special symbols (e.g., *) after some numbers; these symbols provide information about special circumstances. For example the asterisk might indicate that although the data was 100% loaded, it had not yet been fully reviewed by the users. The numbers that are displayed on this report are also useful for several reasons.

First of all, since the report is issued every two weeks, the group's progress is visible on a regular basis. Moreover, this tabular form of status reporting seemed to be a documentation form to which our upper management could easily relate. In addition to using the information for their own analyses, they frequently shared the report with peers and their own management. The progress illustrated in the report was also useful to our users as a vehicle for communication. It enabled the user community to have a handy checklist that depicted exactly how much of their project's data was available at any given time. They found the information especially useful because it was categorized by data type as well as system. It was clearly evident to us that although we may not have been rigorously measuring productivity gains, we were certainly keeping everyone informed in a way they found extremely helpful.

Data Management Status Report as of 8/1/87

Systems	Elements	Interface Records	Data Base Records	User Screens	User Reports
TRS	100%	100%	100%	N/A	N/A
ERS	100%	100%	100%	100%	N/A
PSA *	100%	100%	0%	80%	80%
MAS	100%	100%	100%	100%	100%
SOS	100%	100%	90%	100%	100%
RAS *	100%	100%	0%	80%	80%
ICS *	100%	98%	95%	100%	100%
GLS *	100%	100%	0%	80%	80%

Figure 13–1 Bimonthly status report was useful as a means of communication as well as a measurement of progress.

SIGNIFICANT NUMBERS

We also publicized what I called "significant numbers." For example, we might proudly relate the fact that though we were only three months into the implementation phase, 100% of all the interfaces were loaded into the data dictionary. This was quite an impressive statement, because in effect we were stating that 100% of all the common data was already managed. Another example might be the following: Since the advent of data management, the number of data names used by our system for definition alone has been reduced from 12,000 to 900. (This was absolutely true due to the uncontrolled alias situation.) Did these numbers measure any productivity gain? Probably not, but without doubt they impressed everyone.

TRACKING TRENDS

Since our implementation of Excelerator took place several years later, when we were more sophisticated change agents, we really did make some serious attempts at measuring the improvement. The first technique we employed was what we termed "tracking trends." In our organization, we had a home grown system that tracked and controlled the release management of all our systems. It kept track of the start date, end date, and number of people assigned for every phase of development. Furthermore, this tracking could be reported on an individual user-requested enhancement. A typical report might look like this:

USER REQUEST #23
Movement of Mailbox Function from the
Welcome Screen to the Main Menu.

The purpose of this user request is to allow flexibility in relation to when mail messages are read and deleted. This enhancement will be implemented into all systems during the fourth quarter of this year.

Phase	Start Date	End Date	No. of People Assigned
Definition	2/1	3/15	2
Logical design	3/1	4/15	3
Physical design	4/15	4/30	2
Detailed design	5/1	6/15	4
Code	6/1	8/1	16
Unit test	8/1	8/31	16
System test	9/1	9/30	4
Deploy	10/1	10/15	3

Remarks

On 4/3, all systems are right on target!

We had been utilizing this system for a number of years, before Excelerator was even imagined. As soon as we began our implementation, I not only retained each monthly report, but I went to the system support personnel and got copies of all the reports from the tracking system's first day in production. After we had been using the productivity tool for a full release cycle (2.1), I made some comparisons for every phase of development for each project. I applied the measurement to every phase because by then I had learned the lesson of "you never know who you are buying a tool for." I did not want to overlook the possibility that the most dramatic gain might be, for example, to design/code as opposed to definition, as one would have guessed.

There was indeed an improvement, as can be seen from the diagrams (Figures 13–2a, 13–2b and 13–2c), but I was well aware of all the drawbacks with the measurement. However, I maintained my premise that if there was a substantial and constant improvement in time frames for even one portion of the development life cycle, that might indicate a trend. If the trend was significant and positive, it

Figure 13–2a Time required for definition before Excelerator (up to and including 2.0) and after its implementation (2.1).

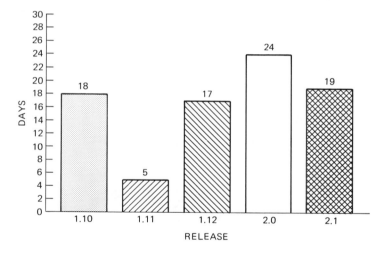

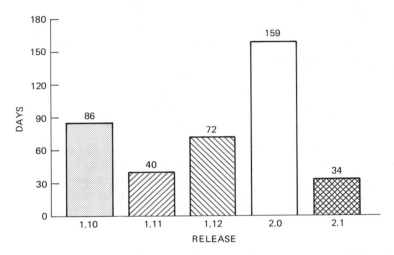

Figure 13–2b Time required for design/code before Excelerator (up to and including 2.0) and after its implementation (2.1).

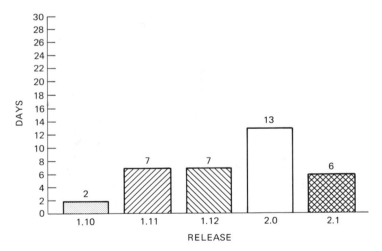

Figure 13–2c Time required for application implementation before Excelerator (up to and including 2.0) and after its implementation (2.1).

could not be summarily dismissed. Finally, it did add to our credibility; we were truly working hard to prove the added value of our mission.

USER SURVEYS

Another approach we took was gathering, compiling, and analyzing what we referred to as the "user view." This is similar to a market research survey of customer satisfaction. We developed a questionnaire which was circulated to all our users; and then we tabulated the results of all the answers we received. The following set of questions is representative of the information you might want to collect:

EXCELERATOR USER SURVEY

1. Which of the following best describes your everyday job function?
   Coding programs   Designing systems   Defining systems
   Testing systems   Support activities   Planning

2. How many years of experience do you have in the field of data processing?

3. Have you personally used Excelerator?

4. If the answer to 3 is yes, how many months?

5. If the answer to 3 is yes, how helpful did you find it?
                Very   Some   Not at All

6. If the answer to 3 is no, would you like to try it?

7. If the answer to 6 is yes, please provide your name.

8. If the answer to 6 is no, please provide a sentence or two that will help us understand your disinterest.
   REASON: _____

9. If you wish to make any comments, please do so in the space provided.
   COMMENTS:_____

It is obvious that many different reports can be generated based on the type of information you gather. For example, client happiness graphed against user type (see Figures 13–3a, 13–3b and 13–3c) or in other words, who appreciates Excelerator more—planners, testers, or analysts?

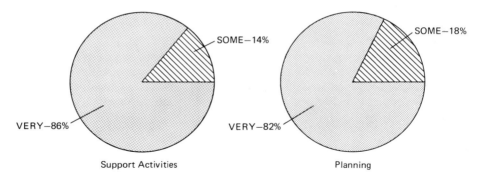

Support Activities

Planning

Figure 13–3a Excelerator user survey: Type of user vs. satisfaction level.

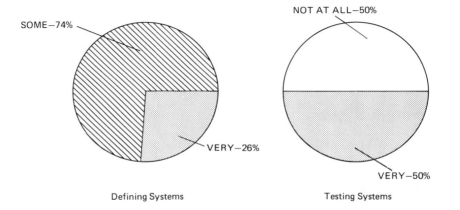

Defining Systems

Testing Systems

Figure 13–3b Excelerator user survey: Type of user vs. satisfaction level.

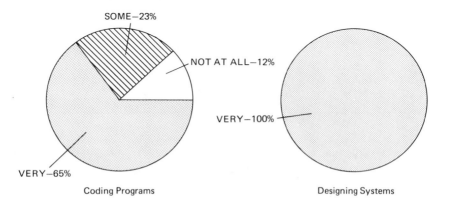

Coding Programs

Designing Systems

Figure 13–3c Excelerator user survey: Type of user vs. satisfaction level.

Another report you could generate might be years of data processing experience versus appreciation (see Figure 13–3d).

Due to our lack of experience, the first user survey we designed had some very interesting peculiarities. For example, we asked people to express interest in receiving information, but neglected to request their names. When we analyzed the results, we were delighted that about 12 of our users had expressed just such a desire. However, since we had not explicitly requested their names, only two people had supplied them unsolicited!

In general, the response to the survey was excellent; and I am convinced that one reason was because it provided an opportunity for people to express themselves anonymously. In the comments section, one responder informed us she hated data processing. We were never quite sure exactly what that and other amusing comments had to do with Excelerator, but we did enjoy them.

The importance of user perception should never be minimized, because no one is in a better position to judge the extent of improvement. Although this method is wholly subjective, it may well prove to be the most useful. Even under adverse circumstances, the overwhelming majority of people do want to perform quality work in an efficient manner. Furthermore, they are not fools and will not knowingly compromise the truth. Therefore, if they firmly believe that quality and quantity have improved, you can be sure that it has.

After our initial implementation of Excelerator, our super user claimed (during a very public presentation) that his project experienced a 50% improvement! He related this increase to the ease with which the group was now able to

Figure 13–3d Relationships between user satisfaction level and years of DP experience.

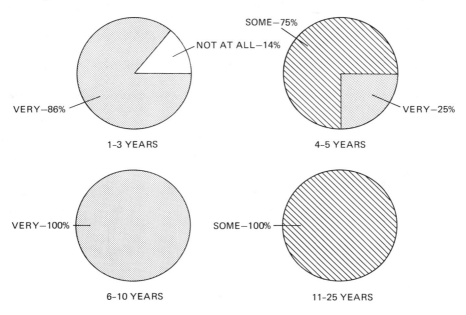

perform the requirements, definition, and logical design phases of development as well as to the fact that much less time and effort were involved. The improvement was almost assuredly not exactly 50%; however, it is a fact it must have been substantial for the project team to have such an impression.

This approach was also quite popular with management, which most likely was related to the political climate of the time. Specifically, we were going through a period when a large factor in determining yearly raises was related to the satisfaction level of each group's customers/users. We had remained attuned to a lesson we learned during our lives as salespeople: Be resourceful and capitalize on all opportunities. Therefore, our survey was well timed and well received.

THE BLIND STUDY

The third alternative, which may well have wide appeal, is a form of the blind study. During the evaluation phase, we had written the business case in the following manner. Remember that we initially believed the greatest and most obvious benefit from this product would be realized during the definition phase of development. Therefore, we compared what was at that time the present reality of how we performed system definition to our projected reality of how we would perform this function using the tool. This comparison included both numbers of days and people. For the people, we applied their loaded salary per day by experience level, as in the sample business case we provided in Chapter 3. Moreover, we performed this quantification for a typical release of the SOS system to which we were assigned at the time. The following extract is from a fictitious business case, but is characteristic of the quantification that was involved:

EXCELERATOR BUSINESS CASE

Assume that typically there are five systems analysts assigned to define an SOS release: one of them is a senior analyst, salary grade 5 (SG5), and three are junior analysts, salary grade 3 (SG3); all salaries are fully loaded. They will be dedicated to this assignment full time for a period of three months. The table indicates the expenditure required for this effort:

Level	No. of People	Annual Compensation	Percent of 1 Yr.	Wage Expense
SG5	1	$61,400	25	$15,350
SG3	3	$51,400	25	$38,550
	TOTAL			$53,900

After the systems analysts gain experience using the tool, we will assume that only one SG5 and one SG3 will be required to define the system. Also assume that they will be assigned to the release full time for a period of six weeks. The following table provides the figures and calculations:

Level	No. of People	Annual Compensation	Percent of 1 Yr.	Wage Expense
SG5	1	$61,400	12.5	$7,675
SG3	1	$51,400	12.5	$6,425
TOTAL				$14,100

It so happened that our first and foremost users were members of the SOS project team and in fact were the people who defined the system for each release. This sophisticated and heavy usage of the tool occurred approximately two years after the original evaluation had been written for upper management approval. Since they had joined our organization about a year into the implementation, they had never set eyes on the business case. During several releases, we asked them to keep track of the amount of time they spent defining the system and to record not only the number of days, but also indicate numbers of people and the experience level or salary grade of each individual. The sample below is illustrative of the actual measurements that were taken by the SOS people and then analyzed by my group:

EXCELERATOR USER MEASUREMENTS

Assume that there were three systems analysts assigned to define the last SOS release: one was a senior analyst (SG5), and two were junior analysts (SG3). They were dedicated to this assignment full time for two months. Although this was a major release of the system, it was not the most substantial one of the year. The SOS people kept track of their own time and provided the numbers used in the calculations below:

Level	No. of People	Annual Compensation	Percent of 1 Yr.	Wage Expense
SG5	1	$61,400	17	$10,438
SG3	2	$51,400	17	$17,476
TOTAL				$27,914

Let's make some comparisons:

Estimated cost at time of original business case without using the tool	$53,900
Projected cost at time of original business case utilizing the tool	$14,100
Actual cost after using the tool	$27,914

Even though the reality of time and numbers of people did not meet the projected ideal environment, the numbers are quite impressive. No one can dispute that it took less time to define the latest version of the SOS system than the original estimation indicated. It is also an obvious (albeit usually unspoken) sentiment that the estimate could be wrong! If the figures are incorrect, then maybe it never did typically take four people three months to define an SOS release. But the real complexity lies in the fact that the estimates could be wrong in either direction. In reality, maybe it usually took six people four months, or maybe it usually took two people one month. Thus it is not merely a question of underestimating or overestimating; the problem is that you are estimating at all.

This quandary might have been avoided by actually measuring at the time of the original business case, but there are problems with that also. The main one lies in the fact that the precision of the measurement is truly questionable; the issues, such as who is doing it and what are the criteria, are not trivial. In the beginning of the chapter we described some of the problems relating to exactly what is being measured. Moreover, in this situation there would also be the issue of who is doing the measurements; one could quite sincerely question their objectivity. For example, if you are describing resources for your project, there might be a tendency to provide the worst case scenario so that you don't find yourself with a reduced staff for the next release. On the other hand, an individual motivated by pride of project might provide the best case scenario.

Moreover, the original projection may have been idealistic, in which case the difference between the estimate and the actual could be more favorable than it appears. However, the main reason that the criticisms remained unuttered was that both the projections and the estimates were made in good faith by people who knew the system. When the measurements were taken, they were not even involved. Furthermore, by now almost everyone (management and users alike) considered themselves part of the process and is feeling quite proud. So in spite of the fact that we have raised numerous questions that reflect seriously on credibility, we still strongly recommend this technique. Be honest about what it truly does and does not demonstrate; but use it and enjoy it, because it probably will be popular.

Before we describe the final measurement method we have used let's summarize:

- In cases such as our data management implementation, a tabular progress report with percentage completed can provide useful status information.
- Any dramatic and significant number should be widely publicized.
- Graphically displaying trends may not be scientific, but if they tend to be consistently positive, cannot be summarily dismissed.
- User surveys will not only provide useful information, but seem to be a pleasant experience for change agents, users, and management.
- Comparing estimates and projections from the original business case to actual statistics gathered by the users provides debatable but interesting results.

UTILIZING TOOLS TO MEASURE QUALITY

The final and perhaps most promising method we are currently pursuing as a way to measure our results is not truly an attempt to measure productivity, but rather an attempt to measure reliability and quality. Moreover, we are utilizing an automated tool, SPQR/20, to predict and measure the defect levels of software projects, the defect removal efficiencies of reviews and tests, as well as the quality and reliability of the delivered software. This tool utilizes Function Point methodology. The method attempts to measure based on a system's five visible attributes: inputs, outputs, data files, inquiries, and interfaces. These attributes are factored for complexity; calculations are performed; and the result is the Function Point Total, which is a number ranging from under a hundred to thousands.

Since the entire object of function points is to measure with a specific number the functionality of systems, they offer a potential vehicle for comparison. For example, this might be a consistent way to measure the relative complexity of two different releases of a system or even the relative complexity of different systems. Although the technique does not address the human factors issues (e.g. system analyst relative competency), it would substantially decrease some of the problems in connection with subjectivity. In fact, there is some capability within SPQR/20 that does attempt to capture the more intangible aspects of productivity; there is an ability to enter user-supplied parameters.

SPQR/20 also considers issues such as whether the programs are new development, enhancements, or maintenance (defect repair), and the extent of the source code's reusability. In terms of available projections, you can obtain predictions about risk of project failure and defect estimates. This defect estimate capability is, in our opinion, where there is some potential for quality assessment— defect severity, testing efficiency, and system reliability and stability. This product can also predict enhancement and defect repair costs. Anyone that is truly concerned with productivity must seriously consider the future maintenance requirements of their systems.

As with all the other methods that have been suggested in this chapter, the real usefulness of tools like SPQR/20 must be evaluated in relation to individual change efforts. However, it is our conviction that the future emphasis on measurement must be in terms of quality. The reason for this emphasis must not be only because it is more possible than measuring productivity, but because it is more important and hence more useful. Indeed, a comparison of the very meaning of the two words is significant. The definition of *productive* is "prolific or yielding favorable or useful results"; while the definition of *quality* is "excellence or superiority." Although being more productive or prolific is surely a worthy goal, producing quality systems that are paradigms of excellence has to be our driving ambition.

SUMMARY

- At this time there is no method to measure productivity improvement that is scientifically acceptable. Most methods are subjective in terms of what is being measured and who is doing the measuring.
- The major problem lies in the difficulty of determining and isolating precisely what it is you are measuring.
- The change process takes a long time, and thus any improvement will appear to be the result of many factors.
- Nevertheless you must attempt to measure some gains, because you began your implementation with projections of benefit. Indeed if you are not curious, your management will be interested.
- The various techniques we have employed are as follows:
  - Progress reports with percentage completed information
  - Publication of significant and dramatic numbers
  - Analysis and graphic depiction of trends
  - Development and analysis of user satisfaction surveys
  - Comparison of original projections and estimations to actual statistics
  - Utilization of tools to measure productivity in terms of quality and reliability

14

Finishing the Implementation: Handling Success

You are now approaching the final stages of finishing the implementation, and although there remain a few tasks for you to perform, primarily your job is completed. You set out on a crusade several years ago; you have passed safely through all the phases of the change process; your effort is totally secure; and you have spent the last year finishing up your mission. You have gently yet unswervingly persisted in your attempt to improve productivity; you have averted several potential disasters; and you have stabilized the situation. The present reality includes a steady increase in usage of the product by the converted and conversion of the uninitiated.

The main caution we offer at this juncture is: Do not become complacent. You may have told your story countless times, but you will still have to give your sales pitch on a regular basis. Moreover, even though you have attained substantial influence and power, you must cherish your original service orientation. Retain some humility; remember how very many people actually did participate to make the present environment a reality.

REMAINING OBJECTIVES

As a matter of fact, it is likely that there are some objectives still to achieve. For example, when we were at this very point in our data management implementation, we still had not assimilated our remote users. To provide some background on this problem, let me describe what I had perceived as one of the fundamental reasons that historically had impeded effective data management in my organization. Namely, our department spanned four separate geographic locations; three of the sites were in the same state, but hundreds of people were thousands of miles away. This substantial distance heightened the usual communication problems associated with the development process, including data management. Our hope was that with an integrated dictionary, electronically accessible to all users, we would be able to compensate for some of these difficulties.

However, our entire implementation approach had been based on utilization of the informal network and hence had consisted of numerous casual, steady social interactions. Therefore, the distance itself had hindered our ability to make any substantial progress in the case of our distant users. We had always been so busy, even during the uneventful phases, that this aspect of the change process had been relegated to the backs of our minds. At this time, though, there was little left to distract us, and we had to face the fact that this was a genuine problem. How we solved it was simple and should have been obvious to us months before. We used the exact same techniques that we had utilized throughout the whole process: We provided information to raise awareness, we listened effectively, we made ourselves available to help, and we held strategy meetings. We began by making a point of visiting our remote users at their location every two weeks for several days at a time.

The first trip we made was not the most pleasant; these users, like all other data processing people, were very busy and not particularly interested in promises of future relief. Since we did not really know any of them personally, there was no resource available to help us with any procedural red tape. For example, we had to make all the arrangements (for meeting rooms, food, etc.) through a centralized conference planning group. Ordinarily, all the phone calls associated with something like this would have been made by one of their secretaries. It was not so much that a major effort was involved, but that it was a sign we were not truly welcome, and that was discouraging. Since people were not all that interested in dealing with us, we did capitalize on some of our newly acquired influence and power. We wrote a memo explaining our function in the organization and our reason for being there. Our management wrote memos to their management requesting cooperation and support. We had our meetings, which were not dramatic in any direction; and we persisted. Finally, by the third trip, although we were by no means close to acceptance, there were some concrete signs of interest. By casual interaction, perhaps something as minor as spotting a screen layout on somebody's desk and offering the information that it was already in our dictionary, we were able to illustrate how we could make life easier. After a few months, we knew our objective had been achieved because they presented us with our own office!

It was also during this time period that we recruited a technical guru into our group, and we were finally in a position to complete our physical implementation. You may recall from Chapter 12 that following our reorganization to the planning division, this work item was relegated to the bottom of our priority list. Its placement was due to the following facts:

- There was a notable lack of resources in terms of people with technical skills available.

- We were dealing with at least a dozen more urgent and critical work items.
- Our users had, in fact, been surviving quite adequately without a local area network.

Common sense dictated that this item could certainly be postponed until there was a more favorable set of circumstances. Now we were finally able to address items such as these, and our own perception of our situation was less constrained. The days of merely trying to ensure the survival of the change process were so far behind us that adding luxuries was now a real possibility. Our technical guru proceeded to implement STARLAN which was impressive enough to be used as a model for other data management groups. In fact, since it consisted solely of our corporation's hardware and software, we actually shared our solution with marketing and selected members of the sales force.

Since you will now have more free time and energy, it will also be possible to provide some additional customized services for your users. In Chapter 9, we described a friend's use of templates during the implementation of Project Workbench. When he arrived at this final stage of his implementation, he extended the concept even further. Not only did he supply each project manager with a template containing all phases and activities of the methodology, but he included a template for the resource spreadsheet he individualized for each project. He prepopulated PW with the names and availability of each person involved, as well as the cost of their labor or their daily rate (see Figures 14–1a and 14–1b).

We provided a similar service for our Excelerator users at this point in our implementation. Although we had instituted version control much earlier in the change effort (see Chapter 9), this was a manual process. At the beginning of the definition phase, we would meet with the project team and jointly determine exactly which records, elements, screens, reports, and data flow diagrams would form the basis for the next release. We mechanized this process by utilizing the entity list feature of Excelerator. Entity lists enable you to create (and retain) a

Project: Project_Life_Cycle_Template

PROJECT-LIFE-CYCLE-TEMPLATE	Da	Who	January 1988 4 11 18 25	February 1988 1 8 15 22 29
RESOURCE SUMMARY				
BARBARA	5.0	BB		
SALLY	5.0	SM		
ALAN	5.0	AS		
KAREN	5.0	KB		
ADAM	5.0	AJ		
TOTAL DAYS				

Figure 14–1a The sample template provides information about each group member's availability (i.e., 5.0 days per week).

FEB 20 88 ACTIVITY STATUS – ACTUAL VS PLAN
PROJECT: PROJECT_LIFE_CYCLE_TEMPLATE

		Start		End			Cost				
Status	CP	Planned	Rev/act	Planned	Rev/act	Who	Actual (+) To-Date	Fcst (=) To-Cmpl	Latest (vs) Estimate	Orig (=) Plan	Ahead (Behind)
RESOURCE SUMMARY											
NAME	RATE										
BARBARA	400					BB	0	0	0	0	0
SALLY	400					SM	0	0	0	0	0
ALAN	200					AS	0	0	0	0	0
KAREN	350					KB	0	0	0	0	0
ADAM	450					AJ	0	0	0	0	0
						Fixd	0	0	0	0	0
TOTAL PROJECT		3-17-88				ALL	0	0	0	0	0
						Fixd	0	0	0	0	0

Figure 14–1b This companion report provides additional information on daily rate (e.g., $450 per day for Adam).

Entity List		SOS Base Line	

Alternate Name Service Order System Rel 0.0
Definition   Starting point for each SOS Release
Next in Chain

Type	Name	Type	Name
DFD	SOS_OVERVIEW	DFD	PROC_ORDER
DFD	ORDER_STAT	DFD	DISTR_ORDER
DMD	POF	DMD	CRDB
REC	SE47	REC	SE11
REC	SE25	REC	SE99
ELE	0110–EQUIPMENT_CODE	ELE	0321–EQUIPMENT_NAME
ELE	1685–EQUIPMENT_QUANTITY	SCD	USER_ENTRY
REP	ORDER_STATUS	TAB	STD_ABBREV

PgDn

Figure 14–2 This sample entity list could be a basis for every SOS release.

group of unrelated items that can be used as the basis for some other activity such as sharing data with other users. Therefore, we created an entity list for each project that would serve as the starting point for each release cycle (see Figure 14–2). Of course, since each release was unique, they invariably had to be modified; but there was always a subset that was constant, so considerable labor was saved.

Naturally, this part of the implementation will be no different from all the earlier phases in the sense that you will continually encounter challenges. However, before we proceed with our discussion, let's list some of the activities you will be performing during this period:

- Completion of objectives that are unpleasant, or not critical, and thus have been artfully ignored, such as our assimilation of remote users
- Attention to tasks that were not essential and consciously relegated a low priority, such as our establishment of a LAN
- Time and energy to expend on luxury items, such as resource spreadsheet templates for Project Workbench and Excelerator entity lists for new releases
- Avoidance of complacency and overutilization of newly acquired political power
- Retention of some measure of humility and continuity of approach

BURNOUT

One of the major challenges that will arise at this time is associated with the un-ending condition of the change process itself. As we indicated at the beginning of this phase, it will never end, and therefore boredom is inevitable, because the process has become monotonous. There is a limit to the number of users you can train, strategy meetings you can hold, and times you can sell upper management. Change agents can suffer from burnout just like other data processing individuals.

It may not be from 80-hour weeks, but rather from the tedium that has begun to be associated with the job. It is, nevertheless, burnout. In fact, it is the very personality of a change agent that will make this situation so unbearable. You are a person who set out to move mountains, and indeed you did. Although when you began, you may not have realized you would do it a shovelful of dirt at a time. In any case, chances are excellent that you are not the type of person who is content when things are peacefully meandering along.

We, not surprisingly, do have some observations and suggestions to share about this inevitable dilemma in the life of a change agent. The real source of the dilemma is that you have been the critical success factor in this whole process; you were from the beginning to the end the one aspect of the implementation that was absolutely essential. It was your assessment of need and firm conviction that began it. It was your knowledge and enthusiasm that sold it. It was your foresight and organizational insight that planned it. It was your drive and your patience that implemented it. It was your dedication and persistence that completed it. Thus, it will not be readily apparent to your management that you are not only restless, but actually no longer essential.

REDEFINING YOUR ROLE

One way you can master this particular condition is to redefine your role. After all, you were the one who created it in the first place, so there is no real reason why you cannot be the one to modify it. The most straightforward way for you to achieve this objective is to expand the scope of your acknowledged function. This is precisely the technique we used in both the data management and Excelerator implementations. In the Excelerator case, we expanded our role to incorporate other tools, such as Project Workbench. Since we were supporting the development process in terms of analysis, it was a natural extension to assume the responsibilities of project planning, control, and tracking.

At first we did meet with some resistance. Our current manager was apprehensive that this expansion of our role would in some way jeopardize our effort. In fact, he held this view so strongly that even the polished and sophisticated salespeople that we had become could not convince him. We were forced to postpone this new role until we were reorganized again. Happily, the next management team was tremendously supportive of our concept of the "integrated developer tool kit." This did precipitate a small flurry of jealousy from some of our peers, but surely we knew the art of overcoming resistance at this stage of the process. In addition, at that time the two vendors were pursuing a seamless interface between their products, which had some implications for us. In particular, the marriage of the two products did lend credibility and support for our newly expanded role. We were invited to and did participate in a planning forum sponsored by both vendors, which did indeed bring some excitement back into our lives as change agents. We were actually afforded the opportunity to provide significant product direction for some of the tools we had been crusading for years to incorporate into everyone's daily work life.

Before we share some additional problems that change agents may encounter during the final months of the process, let's pause and summarize:

- One of the major problems is related to the fact that the change process is unending, and thus boredom is an inevitable consequence for change agents.
- Since you as a change agent have been from the very beginning a critical success factor, the fact that you are no longer essential will not be evident.
- One way to cope with this dilemma is to redefine your role.

INTERACTING WITH CORPORATE GROUPS

Another problem you may experience is some less than positive interactions with various corporate groups. This will vary depending on the quantity and quality of your interactions with them up to this point. If you have had regular information exchanges and have been following their lead, you should not have too much trouble. However, if you have been operating primarily on your own, by the time you come to their attention they may have numerous opinions to express. In either case, since you are in the process of expanding your role, there is a real possibility that intense jealousy (on your part as well as theirs) will enter the picture. But ultimately you must cooperate with these people and establish a reasonably positive relationship.

When we implemented Excelerator, although we did not consciously elect to operate without guidance from our corporate methodology group, that was exactly what occurred. About a year into our implementation, we made our initial contact with them; needless to say, we did not start out in their good graces. They were actually reasonable people who were very competent in their jobs, but the modality of their organization was entirely different from ours. We began our interactions with a series of miscommunications, which resulted in suspicions growing on both sides. They ultimately did give a blessing to our effort, but it took many months and expressions of gentle goodwill on our side to improve our starting position. Once we became better acquainted with some of them, we were also better able to appreciate their viewpoint, and our own resentment abated somewhat. We never did establish a totally positive relationship, but we did arrive at a manageable one.

You must include the corporate groups at some point in your change effort, and you should not be hostile toward them; after all they are just trying to do their jobs. However, timing can be critical. If you involve them too early in the process, they may ensure that your effort is brought to a halt. They are policymakers, and so their timetables will not be as urgent as your own; it is possible that they will advise you to wait months or even years while they study the situation. However, we do not want to imply that their involvement will always be negative. Remember the potential value of their contribution in terms of coordinating employee data across systems (see Chapter 3). You may also recall that when we implemented data management, the corporate standards groups with which we dealt were reasonable and flexible (see Chapter 9). Don't assume that the interactions will be either positive or negative; consider the mentality of your own corporate groups, the extent of possible delay, the urgency of your productivity improvement, the risks in all directions, and then carefully select your moment.

Before we proceed with a discussion of involuntary role expansion, let's recap your group's potential interactions with corporate groups:

- There is a real possibility that as your role expands, your group will clash with various corporate groups.
- You must establish a reasonably positive relationship with all corporate groups.
- This positive relationship will be gained via the same techniques you have applied throughout the entire process—gentle and polite persistence.
- You should attempt to empathize with their perspective and do not prejudge their contribution (or the lack of one).

INVOLUNTARY ROLE EXPANSION

During this period, you may also find your role expanded without any conscious effort on your part. In Chapter 11, we described the elaborate workshops we were offering near the end of our Excelerator implementation. The scope of our training services was communicated quite extensively via the informal network of our attendees. Since we maintained our commitment to cooperation and we valued the extension of our own informal network, we did not limit the workshops to our own users. The result was that we trained people from all over our corporation, gained tremendous visibility, and enjoyed the diversity of our new acquaintances' experiences with the tool.

We also enjoyed some very interesting experiences at the corporate level during the final phases of our data management implementation. As our implementation became more and more a reality, it attracted a reasonable amount of attention. We had many opportunities to participate and provide input to assorted corporate activities. In reality, some of the experiences were more in the category of endurance than enjoyment, particularly those that involved task forces. Our experience indicates that once you become a successful change agent, task force participation or similar activities will require a steadily increasing percentage of your time. We will describe in considerable detail some of the generic difficulties they cause, along with some coping techniques we have employed.

We can certainly all appreciate the significance and importance of gathering people together from dissimilar functional sectors of a company to accomplish a specific task, because there is a similar motivation that drives the formation of the project and interproject teams. However, there are some fundamental differences between task forces and project teams. Task forces are assembled for a specific purpose for a limited amount of time, and there is always an element of urgency. This urgency impedes the formation of a team because there is no magical overnight method for its creation. When the interproject team was being organized (see Chapter 7), considerable effort was expended by the team leader during and between meetings to forge the bond. In reality, the establishment of this team bond is a gradual process, and requires commitment, patience, and persistence on the part of the leader. In the case of the task force, the luxury of time is not an option, and so the gradual process of team building is also not an option.

A further complication lies in the fact that people invariably bring to the task force extreme organizational biases. The organizational pressures are more severe than under ordinary circumstances, because the results of the task force will probably have a profound impact on all the involved organizations. Moreover, there is considerable pressure to produce a useful deliverable quickly. These two facts tend to cause substantial conflict for task force members who must reconcile corporate objectives and their organizational allegiances. Finally, the fact that you must be away from your regular assignment for an undetermined amount of time tends to promote frustration even before the first meeting. You will have to arrange for your group to be managed while you are absent and then somehow ensure that it is managed well. All these factors foster an atmosphere of relentlessness and intensity in task forces that always made me classify them as cruel and unusual punishment.

How do you deal with this fairly unpleasant situation that you as a successful change agent are likely to be in more than once? In relation to the team issues, you must attempt to promote a team bond; in this case, however, you will not be the leader, but rather a participant. You may not find this role altogether comfortable. After all, as the principal change agent, you have been in charge of things for quite a while. Now, instead of directing an effort, you are being asked to participate in it. The first step toward achieving this goal is to recognize and accept this role as the capacity in which you will be serving the task force. Once you adapt yourself, you might find the experience quite pleasurable. Consider the activities that have become boring that you will not have to perform, such as selling and teaching. All you have to do is effectively listen, evaluate what is happening (interpersonal dynamics as well as events), and when necessary contribute. It is another matter altogether to address the political realities, such as serving true corporate need while adequately representing your own organization. Personally speaking I always harbored the fear that upon my return my management would demand accusingly: "How could you have let this happen?" It was never clear to me whether the accusation was because the product of the task force was mediocre or because our organization's interests had suffered. In either case, I was convinced there would be trouble. So what is the solution? The secret lies in remaining truly open-minded.

Being open-minded involves utilizing both communication skills—listening and speaking—plus an additional ingredient. You must listen effectively, present your point of view, and then carefully weigh what is being said against your own beliefs. This is never easy for us, because it causes some internal conflict; it is even more difficult when we are also being influenced by politics. It is so much simpler to doggedly hold onto our organization's viewpoint by convincing ourselves that this is our own view as well as the right one. (People will often stubbornly retain a position in the face of overwhelmingly contradictory information.) However, what you must do after you have listened to all points of view is to weigh each one against your own experience.

The result will be the solution to the dilemma, but you are not quite finished yet; you must also evaluate your organization's reaction to it. If you cannot sell the result to your management, then you must attempt get the group to modify it enough so that it will be acceptable to your people. Remember in this situation "buy in" is an objective for the task force leader, just as it was for you with your interproject team. It will therefore most assuredly be an objective to assist you in your desire to gain your management's acceptance. Figure 14–3 provides a road map of the process.

The final hardship is that task force participation taxes your ability to be a good manager. This ability really calls for the application of two techniques; keeping your group going and keeping your management informed. Keeping your group going from a distance is not as troublesome as you might suppose. You should leave your most trusted and dependable staff member in charge. This individual is not necessarily the one with the most seniority or experience. Don't worry about selecting the right one either, because you have had substantial experience in sizing them up for different functions

Figure 14–3   Being open-minded will ensure the success of the task force.

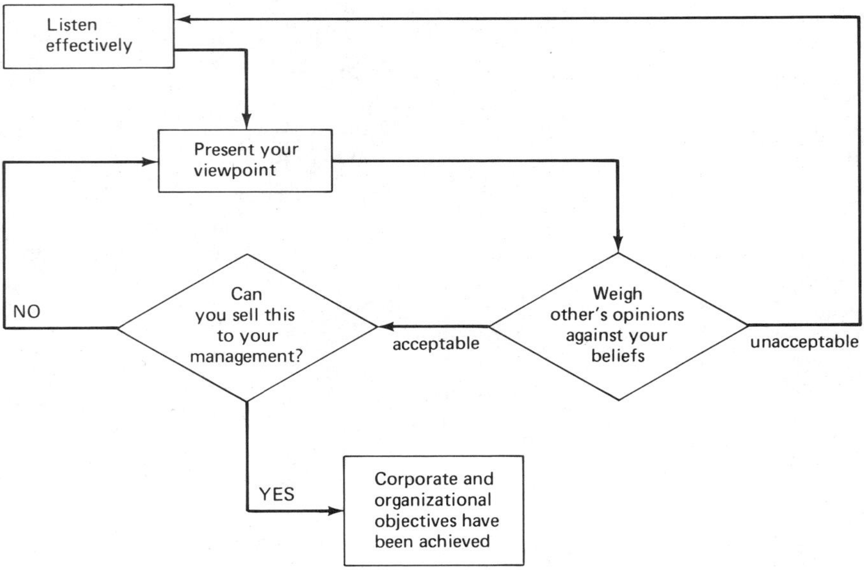

(see Chapters 3 and 12). Then ensure that you can always be reached in a crisis. Furthermore, you will call regularly in order to maintain the group's team bond. This act of connecting is similar to one of the techniques you used to maintain the interproject team bond between meetings. Finally, avoid fretting about what is happening (or not happening). Even if the situation becomes truly muddled, you can sort it all out upon your return.

To keep your boss informed, you should utilize the same techniques: ensure that he can reach you, and call him regularly. In addition, it is usually a good idea to send memos that serve the function of task force status reports from your perspective. Include the events that have taken place, the areas addressed by the task force that you feel comfortable with, and anything that is a major concern to you. In connection with sharing concerns, we are not suggesting hysteria. There may be an area where you are dissatisfied with the group's decisions and you eloquently shared your concerns. If the group members refuse to alter their plans, there is no advantage in keeping this to yourself. Your boss may respond with some very specific instructions, such as ignore this issue or resurface your concerns resolutely; or he may ignore the issue entirely. In any case you have expressed yourself formally for the record, and you have not disrupted the group's efforts by dwelling on this item.

Since involuntary role expansion will undoubtedly increase as you become a successful change agent, let's attempt to distill some of its most significant aspects:

- As you become successful, you will find yourself involved more and more often in corporate activities such as task forces.
- Task forces bear some similarity to interproject teams, but the gradual building of team bond is seldom possible in the task force situation.
- You can contribute to the establishment of a team bond by recognizing that you are not the leader but a participant and utilizing your acquired skills (e.g., effective listening) to be useful in this role.
- Every participant must resolve the conflict of serving true corporate need while adequately representing the needs of their own organization.
- In order to reconcile this conflict between corporate and organizational goals, you must be open-minded.
- Another hardship caused by task force participation is the difficulty of being a good manager in absentia.
- To ensure your group's well-being while you are away, remain accessible to your delegated authority and your manager, and also contact them regularly to maintain the group bond.

THE END OF THE ROAD

We have just about come to the end of our journey down the road of productivity improvement. As a final example, we would like to share the story of how we handled the change agent burnout dilemma in our data management implementation.

We were at the point where our data was finally under control; no new aliases were being created, and in fact no elements were being added, deleted, or modified without first being analyzed by my group. We were considering various ways to extend this control into the software itself, when a programmer suggested a feasible way for us to proceed. The recommendation was to repeat the same process we had employed in gaining control of our logical view of the data—namely, to begin changing the physical reality with the interfaces, which was the least complex, and work gradually toward the problems that would be involved in changing IMS databases. Not only did I consider this a brilliant suggestion, but I was overjoyed at concrete evidence of the extent that we had succeeded in overcoming resistance. How many times can any of us boast that we have precipitated a programmer's actually volunteering to modify code? However, we did not proceed with the recommendation, although we seriously considered it. We decided the effort was just not worth the result. This was the very moment when we brainstormed our way to the modern data architecture of a conceptual data model and the subject databases. We reached the vision of a more proactive role; we did not merely want to administer the data, but rather to shape it into a stable structure that would accurately reflect our business needs.

I placed my most promising acolyte in charge of this effort, and the plan unfolded. We would follow the same steps we had taken to implement data management; that is, we would proceed with every phase of the change process from the beginning. We had already assessed a need—namely, our basic architecture was unstable because each system had its own version of the same data. What was required was not an SOS database, an ERS database, etc., but an employee data base, a customer data base, etc. The next step would involve an evaluation, which would include a business case. Then the marketing phase could begin. My protege would have to sell upper management as well as the potential users. There would be a period of information gathering, during which the new change agents would listen, analyze, and brainstorm their way to an approach. The planning phase would cry out for an interproject team to develop a migration strategy and schedule. The programmers would offer the technical guidance; the systems analysts would schedule (nondisruptively) their recommendations into planned releases; and the strategic planners would keep everyone informed of possible future end user needs and factor the proposed migration plans in with end user priorities.

I had chosen my successor, and began preparing her to be a missionary on this new crusade. I started my search for the next role I would assume as a change agent. When the effort was well underway, and our management had a high degree of confidence in her and in this new productivity improvement, I proceeded to my next crusade.

SUMMARY

- Although you are nearing the end of the change process, you cannot become complacent. Work items that had a low priority still need to be completed.

- You can also make use of the free time and energy to provide some additional customized services for your users.
- The major problem that will arise at this stage is the change agent's burnout. This phenomenon is associated with the unending condition of the change process itself.
- The personality of the change agent will undoubtedly contribute to the burnout, but can also be utilized to reshape his or her role.
- The redefinition of role may be accomplished in several ways (e.g., incorporation of new productivity tools) and may in some cases even be involuntary (e.g., task force participation).

Bibliography

References contained in this bibliography fall into two distinct categories. One group provides reading material that has inspired me on the subjects of the philosophy, necessity, and process of change. Other references expand on themes discussed in *Agents of Change* or offer supplementary information on peripheral subjects essential to the process of implementing change.

CHANGE—PHILOSOPHY, NECESSITY, and PROCESS REFERENCES

BROOKS, FREDERICK P. *The Mythical Man-Month: Essays on Software Engineering*, Reading, Mass.: Addison-Wesley, 1975.

CARTWRIGHT, DORWIN AND ALVIN ZANDER, *Group Dynamics: Research in Theory*, Evanston, Ill.: Row, Peterson and Company, 1953.

DRUCKER, PETER F., *The Age of Discontinuity: Guidelines to Our Changing Society*, New York: Harper & Row, 1969.

GEIS, GEORGE T. AND KUHN, ROBERT L., *Micromanaging: Transforming Business Leaders with Personal Computers*, Englewood Cliffs, N.J.: Prentice-Hall, 1987.

HARE, PAUL AND EDGAR F. BORGATTA AND ROBERT F. BATES, *Small Groups: Studies in Social Interaction*, New York: Alfred A. Knopf, 1955.

KIDDER, TRACY, *The Soul of a New Machine*, New York: Little-Brown, 1981.

KUHN, THOMAS S., *The Structure of Scientific Revolutions*, Chicago, Ill.: University of Chicago Press, 1962.

MARTIN, JAMES, *Strategic Data-Planning Methodologies*, Englewood Cliffs, N.J.: Prentice-Hall, 1982.

PETERS, TOM AND NANCY AUSTIN, *A Passion for Excellance: The Leadership Difference*, New York: Random House, 1985.

PIRSIG, ROBERT, *Zen and the Art of Motorcycle Maintenance*, New York: Bantam Books, 1975.

TOFFLER, ALVIN, *Future Shock*, New York: Random House, 1972.

WEINBERG, GERALD M., *The Psychology of Computer Programming*, New York: Van Nostrand Reinhold Company, 1971.

YOURDON, EDWARD, *Nations at Risk: The Impact of the Computer Revolution*, New York: Yourdon Press, 1986.

ZVEGINTZOV, NICHOLAS, *Software Maintenance News*.

CHANGE—RELATED AND PHERIPHERAL REFERENCES

ANDRE, RAE AND PETER D. WARD, *The :59–Second Employee: How to Stay One Second Ahead of Your One Minute Manager*, Boston, Mass.: Houghton Mifflin Company, 1984.

BLOCK, ROBERT, *The Politics of Projects*, New York: Yourdon Press, 1983.

BUSKIRK, RICHARD H., *Handbook of Managerial Tactics*, Boston, Mass.: Cahners Books, 1976.

COHEN, HERB, *You Can Negotiate Anything: How to Get What You Want*, Secaucus, N.J.: Citadel Press, 1980.

DEMARCO, T. AND T. LISTER, *Peopleware: Productive Projects and Teams*, New York: Dorset House Publishing Company, 1987.

EMERY, DAVID A., *The Complete Manager*, New York: McGraw-Hill Book Company, 1970.

FRANK, MILO O., *How to Get Your Point Across in 30 Seconds—or Less*, New York: Simon and Schuster, 1986.

GORDON, MYRON, *How to Plan and Conduct a Successful Meeting*, New York: Sterling Publishing Company, 1981.

HERSEY, PAUL AND KEN BLANCHARD, *Management of Organizational Behavior: Utilizing Human Resources*, Englewood Cliffs, N.J.: Prentice-Hall, 1982.

JOHNSON, SPENCER AND LARRY WILSON, *The One Minute Sales Person*, New York: William Morrow and Company, 1984.

JONES, CAPERS, *Programming Productivity*, New York: McGraw-Hill Book Company, 1986.

KREPNER, CHARLES H. AND BENJAMIN B. TREGOR, *The New Rational Manager*, Ptincton, N.J.: Princeton Research Press, 1981.

LEVY, FERDINAND K., AND JEROME D. WIEST, *A Management Guide to PERT/CPM: with GERT/DCPM and other Networks*, Englewood Cliffs, N.J.: Prentice-Hall, 1977.

SEMPREVIVO, PHILIP C., *Teams in Information Systems Development*, New York: Yourdon Press, 1980.

STEWART, NATHANIEL, *Help Your Boss & Help Yourself*, New York: AMACOM, 1974.

THOMAS, DAVID A. AND MARIDELL FRYAR, *Successful Business Speaking: A Practical Guide for the Student and Professional*, Skokie, Ill.: National Textbook Company, 1981.

WESTON, J. FRED AND EUGENE F. BRIGHAM, *Managerial Finance*, Hinsdale, Ill.: Dryden Press, 1972.

WILLIAMSON, PORTER B., *Patton's Principles: A Handbook for Managers Who Mean It!*, New York: Simon and Schuster, 1979.

INDEX

YOU HAVE TAKEN THE FIRST STEP
NOW TAKE THE NEXT STEP

We wrote the book! Bouldin, Inc. also provides educational and consulting services.

For information contact us at:

    201-221-9498   or

Detach this form, fill in the necessary information and mail to:

Bouldin, Inc.
31 Ambar Place
Bernardsville, NJ
07924

NAME   _____

COMPANY   _____

ROOM   _____

STREET   _____

CITY   _____ STATE _____ ZIP _____

PHONE   _____

TEAR OUT THIS PAGE TO ORDER THESE OTHER HIGH-QUALITY YOURDON PRESS COMPUTING SERIES TITLES

Quantity	Title/Author	ISBN	Price	Total $
_____	Building Controls Into Structured Systems; Brill	013-086059-X	$35.00	_____
_____	C Notes: Guide to C Programming; Zahn	013-109778-4	$21.95	_____
_____	Classics in Software Engineering; Yourdon	013-135179-6	$39.00	_____
_____	Concise Notes on Software Engineering; DeMarco	013-167073-3	$21.00	_____
_____	Controlling Software Projects; DeMarco	013-171711-1	$39.00	_____
_____	Creating Effective Software; King	013-189242-8	$33.00	_____
_____	Crunch Mode; Boddie	013-194960-8	$29.00	_____
_____	Current Practices in Software Development; King	013-195678-7	$34.00	_____
_____	Data Factory; Roeske	013-196759-2	$23.00	_____
_____	Developing Structured Systems; Dickinson	013-205147-8	$34.00	_____
_____	Design of On-Line Computer Systems; Yourdon	013-201301-0	$48.00	_____
_____	Essential Systems Analysis; McMenamin/Palmer	013-287905-0	$35.00	_____
_____	Expert System Technology; Keller	013-295577-6	$28.95	_____
_____	Concepts of Information Modeling; Flavin	013-335589-6	$27.00	_____
_____	Game Plan for System Development; Frantzen/McEvoy	013-346156-4	$30.00	_____
_____	Intuition to Implementation; MacDonald	013-502196-0	$24.00	_____
_____	Managing Structured Techniques; Yourdon	013-551037-6	$33.00	_____
_____	Managing the System Life Cycle 2/e; Yourdon	013-551045-7	$35.00	_____
_____	People & Project Management; Thomsett	013-655747-3	$23.00	_____
_____	Politics of Projects; Block	013-685553-9	$24.00	_____
_____	Practice of Structured Analysis; Keller	013-693987-2	$28.00	_____
_____	Program It Right; Benton/Weekes	013-729005-5	$23.00	_____
_____	Software Design: Methods & Techniques; Peters	013-821828-5	$33.00	_____
_____	Structured Analysis; Weinberg	013-854414-X	$44.00	_____
_____	Structured Analysis & System Specifications; DeMarco	013-854380-1	$44.00	_____
_____	Structured Approach to Building Programs: BASIC; Wells	013-854076-4	$23.00	_____
_____	Structured Approach to Building Programs: COBOL; Wells	013-854084-5	$23.00	_____
_____	Structured Approach to Building Programs: Pascal; Wells	013-851536-0	$23.00	_____
_____	Structured Design; Yourdon/Constantine	013-854471-9	$49.00	_____
_____	Structured Development Real-Time Systems, Combined; Ward/Mellor	013-854654-1	$75.00	_____
_____	Structured Development Real-Time Systems, Vol. 1; Ward/Mellor	013-854787-4	$33.00	_____
_____	Structured Development Real-Time Systems, Vol. II; Ward/Mellor	013-854795-5	$33.00	_____
_____	Structured Development Real-Time Systems, Vol. III; Ward/Mellor	013-854803-X	$33.00	_____
_____	Structured Systems Development; Orr	013-855149-9	$33.00	_____
_____	Structured Walkthroughs 3/e; Yourdon	013-855248-7	$24.00	_____
_____	System Development Without Pain; Ward	013-881392-2	$33.00	_____
_____	Teams in Information System Development; Semprivivo	013-896721-0	$29.00	_____
_____	Techniques of EDP Project Management; Brill	013-900358-4	$33.00	_____
_____	Techniques of Program Structure & Design; Yourdon	013-901702-X	$44.00	_____
_____	Up and Running; Hanson	013-937558-9	$32.00	_____
_____	Using the Structured Techniques; Weaver	013-940263-2	$27.00	_____
_____	Writing of the Revolution; Yourdon	013-970708-5	$38.00	_____
_____	Practical Guide to Structured Systems 2/e; Page-Jones	013-690769-5	$35.00	_____

Total $ _____

Discount (if appropriate) _____

New Total $ _____

AND TAKE ADVANTAGE OF THESE SPECIAL OFFERS!

a.) When ordering 3 or 4 copies (of the same or different titles), take 10% off the total list price (excluding sales tax, where applicable).

b.) When ordering 5 to 20 copies (of the same or different titles), take 15% off the total list price (excluding sales tax, where applicable).

c.) To receive a greater discount when ordering 20 or more copies, call or write:

Special Sales Department
College Marketing
Prentice Hall
Englewood Cliffs, NJ 07632
201-592-2498

SAVE!

If payment accompanies order, plus your state's sales tax where applicable, Prentice Hall pays postage and handling charges. Same return privilege refund guaranteed. Please do not mail in cash.

☐ **PAYMENT ENCLOSED**—shipping and handling to be paid by publisher (please include your state's tax where applicable).

☐ **SEND BOOKS ON 15-DAY TRIAL BASIS** & bill me (with small charge for shipping and handling).

Name _____

Address _____

City _____ State _____ Zip _____

I prefer to charge my ☐ Visa ☐ MasterCard
Card Number _____ Expiration Date_____

Signature _____
All prices listed are subject to change without notice.

Mail your order to: Prentice Hall, Book Distribution Center, Route 59 at
Brook Hill Drive, West Nyack, NY 10995

Dept. 1   D-OFYP-FW(1)